# Washington, D.C.

## YESTERDAY & TODAY ™

Rosanne C. Scott

WEST
SIDE
PUBLISHING

**Rosanne C. Scott** is a freelance writer and editor and a longtime Washingtonian. She has written for Time-Life Books and AARP, among others. She has also helped American and European visitors make the most of their trips to the nation's capital as a writer and editor for the London-based *Insight Guides: Washington, D.C.,* travel series. She lives with her husband near George Washington's Mt. Vernon estate.

Facts verified by **Betsy Rossen Elliot.**

Yesterday & Today is a trademark of Publications International, Ltd.

West Side Publishing is a division of Publications International, Ltd.

Louis Weber, CEO
Publications International, Ltd.
7373 North Cicero Avenue
Lincolnwood, Illinois 60712

Permission is never granted for commercial purposes.
ISBN-13: 978-1-60553-917-1
ISBN-10: 1-60553-917-1

Manufactured in China.

8 7 6 5 4 3 2 1

Library of Congress Control Number: 2010923318

This African elephant, which weighed 12 tons when it was killed in 1955, dominates the rotunda at the Smithsonian's National Museum of Natural History.

# Contents

# Capital City Built on Compromise

As John Kennedy once quipped, Washington, D.C., is a city of Southern efficiency and Northern charm, a wisecrack reference to the story of the capital's founding—a story that naturally involves politics and money. Fresh from their win over the British in 1783, the founders turned almost immediately to squabbling over where to put the capital.

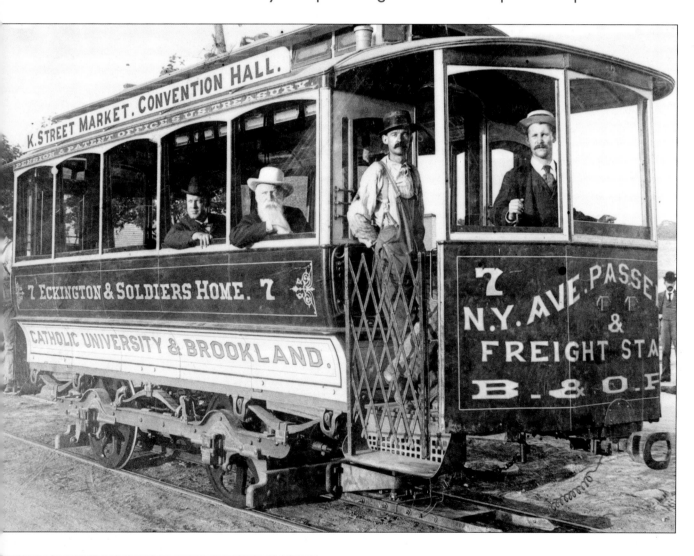

Wealthy Southern planters faced off against stubborn Northerners: The Southerners had paid their share of the then-staggering $50 million Revolutionary War debt up front and wanted the capital in their neck of the woods; however, the Northerners, who had borne more of the cost, still held most of the debt and refused to budge on the capital question until the federal government agreed to assume their load. Thomas Jefferson and Treasury secretary Alexander Hamilton eventually brokered a win-win deal that covered the war debt with a new bond issue. They put the capital, a 100-square-mile federal district, in neither the north nor the south but along the Potomac River between Maryland and Virginia with each area contributing real estate. (In 1846, Virginia asked for and got its

In 1900, this particular streetcar carried passengers between Brookland, in the east, and downtown's K Street. Most lines had been electrically powered since the late 1800s, though some were still horse drawn into the 20th century.

acreage back, which accounts for the city's present-day jagged southwestern border.) With their part finished, they left the shaping of this new capital to George Washington, who turned to Major Pierre-Charles L'Enfant for help. L'Enfant was a Frenchman who had served in the Continental Army. He was trained as an architect, and his vision for what was indeed America's first planned community incorporated broad avenues and monumental public buildings on par with ancient Greece and Rome. Though brilliant, L'Enfant was also temperamental. In fact, he was so cantankerous that Washington fired him within a year. A patchwork of architects and builders followed, but the nation's capital languished for years.

Then, in August 1814, the British came back. America's objections over the illegal impress of its sailors into the British navy had sparked the War of 1812, prompting the British to invade Washington and torch the White House and the Capitol, which had been more or less complete. For once, Washington's legendary equatorial summer weather turned out to be a good thing. A sudden tropical downpour doused the flames, but the city was in ruin—in the following decades, as the government bureaucracy expanded, construction couldn't keep pace.

## LIVING UP TO ITS TITLE
At the beginning of the Civil War, there were 2,200 federal employees. Ten years later, in 1871, that number had tripled. Between 1860 and 1877, the city's population swelled from 75,000 to

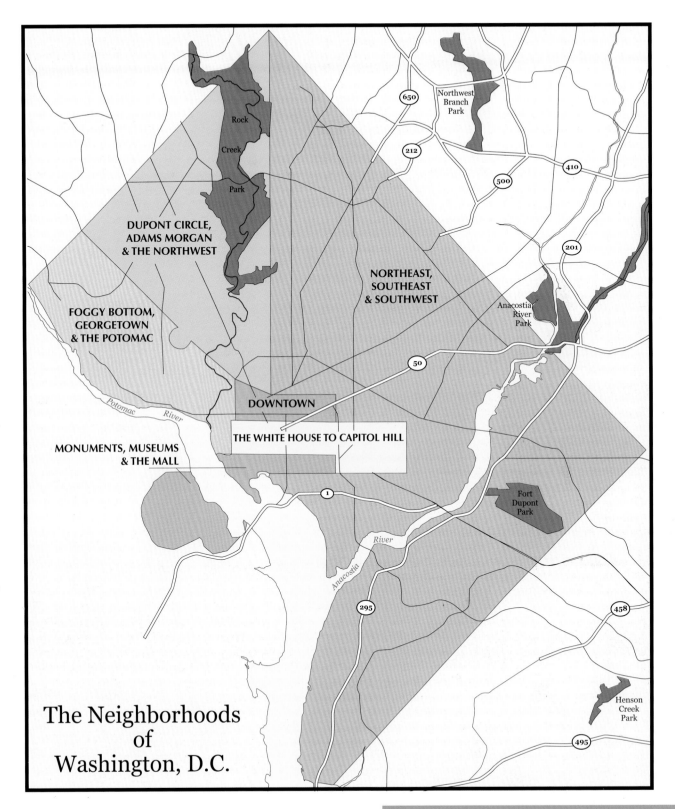

The Neighborhoods
of
Washington, D.C.

175,000, but Washington was ill equipped to provide even basic city services.

Slaughterhouse refuse flowed in the streets, shacks lined L'Enfant's boulevards, and what passed for a sewage system basically amounted to a foul ditch that carried waste into the Potomac when the tide wasn't pushing it back. There was so much mud, stench, and crime that a movement arose to move the capital to a more civilized place, such as St. Louis or Cincinnati. But the end of the Civil War brought the city new legitimacy: Hub of the Union war effort, Washington had managed to save the nation and with that triumph came a sense that America's destiny, whatever it may be, should issue forth from its capital. Fueled by its newfound pride, Washington paved, drained, lit, and landscaped itself in a whirlwind first round of civic improvement.

Today, Washington, D.C., is every American's city, a sort of national hometown. Compared to most American cites, however, it's small—only about 61 square miles—and its citizens number fewer than 600,000 (although there are more than five million in the metro area). Most arrive from elsewhere—here to serve in government or in a business that supports it, many only until the next election or until a government contract runs out. Those who do stay on and become full-fledged Washingtonians settle into a city that has no distinctive ethnic culture and no regional accent or cuisine. Full of politicians and people who love policy, Washington lives by its stodgy reputation. Trendy restaurants are few, its nightlife lackluster, but its social scene is world-renowned and includes glamorous inaugural balls, White House state dinners, and posh Georgetown receptions. The Kennedy Center, which is the major performing arts venue, hardly stacks up against New York's Broadway, but Washington, D.C., also has the Smithsonian Institution and National Gallery of Art, which are home to many of the world's treasures—and available for everyone to enjoy for free. Any city where visitors can see Rothko, da Vinci, the Hope Diamond, and the winged contraption that first sent the Wright brothers aloft—all in a single afternoon, without spending a dime—can't be all bad.

## PROVING PEOPLE WRONG

Critics claim that Washington's preoccupation with granite and marble imbues the place with an air of pomposity. It is true that there's hardly a street corner without a monument to a person or event, no matter how insignificant. Unlike most cities, though, there are no

The Smithsonian's Air and Space Museum features the world's first airplane, the Wright brothers' Flyer, seen here today. The museum opened in 1976 to coincide with the nation's bicentennial and is reputed to be the world's most visited. Among its extensive holdings are Charles Lindbergh's *Spirit of St. Louis,* in which the aviator made the first transatlantic crossing; the *Enola Gay,* from which the first atomic bomb was dropped; and the Apollo 11 command module *Columbia,* used in the moon landing.

skyscrapers, due to a long-standing law restricting building height, which also means it is free from sunless, desolate urban canyons. Add to that Washington's leafy Rock Creek Park and its Potomac gushing over Great Falls and you have one of the world's most beautiful cities.

Many also complain about the politics, and there's hardly a congressman or senator, especially before an election, who doesn't claim the need to get out of Washington and back to the "real" America, as if the city were foreign territory. As any of the millions of visitors who flock here every year will say, Washington *is* the real America. It is a city distinctly shaped by the nation's history, both glorious and terrible. It is leading the nation toward its future, and since the city's founding in 1790, it has been a beacon of hope for the world. And for those who still have doubts, the words from Lincoln's second inaugural address carved into the wall of the Lincoln Memorial say it all: "With malice toward none, with charity for all, with firmness in the right as God gives us to see the right, let us strive on to finish the work we are in. . . . "

Nothing says "4th of July" like the Washington Monument, seen here against a sky sparkling with fireworks.

## The White House to Capitol Hill

# Power and Progress on Pennsylvania Avenue

Standing on the pedestrian stretch of Pennsylvania Avenue in front of the White House and looking through the iron fence, one is surprised by how small the president's house seems in relation to the power and influence concentrated there. City planner Pierre L'Enfant's original idea called for something palatial, something befitting a king, but George Washington had no kingly intentions. The Revolutionary War, after all, had ushered in the era of the "citizen-statesman"—emphasis on "citizen"—and whatever shape the president's house might take, its resident was only there temporarily.

The Capitol, the true center of the people's government, was the real focus, and to reflect its importance, L'Enfant chose Jenkins Hill, the highest point in the city, on which to erect it. Linking the White House and the Capitol is that famous one-mile stretch of Pennsylvania Avenue, named for the state as a sort of consolation prize when Philadelphia lost its bid for capital city status. Although L'Enfant envisioned it as a grand boulevard filled with high-end shops and residences, Pennsylvania Avenue and its adjacent blocks were mostly a jumble of government offices, busy meat and produce markets, and crowded shanties and brothels until well into the 20th century. Improvement was gradual and involved demolishing the thriving Center Market (in operation from 1801 to 1931) to make way for the National Archives—the repository of the nation's most important documents—and clearing the notorious Murder Bay to make way for Federal Triangle, a stylish complex of government office buildings begun in the 1930s and finally completed in the 1990s. The ingeniously wedge-shape Canadian Embassy and the Newseum, a museum devoted exclusively to journalism,

St. John's Episcopal Church (shown here in 1923) is also known as "The Church of the Presidents" due to the number of presidents who have worshipped here over the years.

*Opposite:* This 1920s photograph of Pennsylvania Avenue was taken from 9th Street, with the Capitol building in the distance.

The Library of Congress's Main Reading Room, shown here today, rises 160 feet above the mahogany desks on the first level to a cupola of stained glass that, on sunny days, lights this grand space with rays of color. Eight massive columns encircle the room, each topped with figures symbolizing art, commerce, history, law, philosophy, poetry, religion, and science.

are the avenue's newest additions, making its beautification complete—Pennsylvania Avenue is at last worthy of being called "America's Main Street."

## THE WHITE HOUSE NEIGHBORHOOD

The White House, or President's House as it was originally known, is the oldest public building in the city. It was designed by architect James Hoban (chosen from among eight other architects in competition), who drew on the grand manor houses of his native Ireland for inspiration. Construction began in October 1792, but rising costs, plan modifications, and a lack of skilled workmen made the going slow—so slow, in fact, that when George Washington died in 1799, the house still wasn't finished, making Washington the only

president never to have lived in it. Thomas Jefferson, ever the architect, modified and improved the house, adding formal gardens and serpentine walkways. Thus, by the time James Madison and his fashionable wife, Dolley, arrived in 1809, the President's House had finally evolved into a stately manse. That is, until one steamy August night in 1814, during the War of 1812, when the British stormed Washington and burned the house nearly to the ground.

Rebuilding was swift—perhaps too swift, because more than once, shortcuts nearly caused the building to collapse. Thus, during the Truman administration, it was gutted and refitted. Meanwhile, in adjacent Lafayette Square, Washington's elite were building elegant new homes,

including Blair House (eventually the guest house for presidential visitors) and Decatur House, the home of the naval hero Stephen Decatur. When Washington residents weren't attending services at St. John's Episcopal Church—opened just across the square in 1816, where many presidents have since worshipped—they were admiring the art around the corner at the Renwick, the city's first gallery, which opened in 1859 and is now part of the Smithsonian.

Perhaps the grandest addition to the neighborhood, though, was a government office building, erected in 1888 in the ornate style known as Second Empire. It served as headquarters for the State, War, and Navy departments until it was annexed in 1947 and turned into presidential office space. Resembling a wedding cake, with all its tiers and trim, it's known today as the Old Executive Office Building and stands next door to the comparatively modest President's House or, as it's been known since Teddy Roosevelt's time, the White House. The house had always been painted white, but it was Roosevelt who engraved his stationery with the name, thereby making it official.

## CAPITOL HILL

As for the Capitol, construction began in 1793 and quickly devolved into an early example of Washington infighting. One architect after another signed on to the project and then quit, having clashed with either frustrated construction engineers (who, in some cases, were better trained than the architects themselves) or with Congress (whose members seemed to forget that the Capitol was not their monument but a place for the people's business). By 1800, enough of the Capitol had been completed to allow Congress to meet there for the first time. But, just like the White House, the British torched it when they stormed Washington in 1814. The Capitol was rebuilt, of course, but by 1850, as more states joined the Union, Congress needed a bigger building—essentially the one that exists today. In 2008, the Capitol Visitors Center opened to accommodate the nearly 20,000 people

who arrive every day, and the center's exhibits and theaters are geared toward arming them with a better understanding of how our government works. An engineering marvel, it's completely underground so as not to mar the character of the Hill, a neighborhood that, with a few notable exceptions, is composed of 19th-century Federal-style townhouses whose exteriors are little changed. Eastern Market, an old-style fresh food emporium and flea market—and the center of local life on the Hill—has been in operation since 1873. Its red brick modesty doesn't compare to the Library

of Congress, however, which is a Beaux-Arts gem that opened across the street from the Capitol in 1897; it's arguably the city's most beautiful building. In 1932, it was joined by the Folger Shakespeare Library, which contains the world's largest collection of Shakespeare's printed work. And in 1935, after meeting in taverns, private homes, and even the Capitol itself for the first 145 years of its history, the U.S. Supreme Court finally got a home of its own just east of the Capitol, its imposing marble pediment inscribed with these familiar words: "Equal Justice Under Law."

A modern-day, aerial view of Washington, D.C., shows the Capitol in its place of prominence on the Hill.

# THE WHITE HOUSE

Gerald Ford called it "the best public housing I've ever seen," and Ronald Reagan likened it to an eight-star hotel. Even so, the White House is modest compared with the homes of many other heads of state.

The White House has 132 rooms, including the State Dining Room, which seats 140, and the East Room, a formal reception area. A full-length Gilbert Stuart portrait of George Washington (the only object original to the house) hangs in the East Room, and presidents Lincoln and Kennedy have lain in state there.

The East Room was also the site of wrestling matches staged for the amusement of Teddy Roosevelt and where Richard Nixon delivered his resignation speech in 1974.

The Oval Office, of course, is world-famous. It was completed in 1909 and was first occupied by William Howard Taft. But the other best-known room in the White House may be Lincoln's bedroom—he never slept in it, but he used it as an office. And on New Year's Day 1863, he signed the Emancipation Proclamation there, officially ending slavery.

Until well into the 20th century, the White House was open to the public, and the president was surprisingly accessible. However, in the 1930s, Herbert Hoover quit the custom of receiving uninvited visitors, and security concerns that began with the onset of World War II (which closed the roads that flank the White House) only increased in the decades that followed. Finally, after the attacks of September 11, 2001, the White House was closed to everyone but special tour groups, and Pennsylvania Avenue, in front of the mansion, is now permanently inaccessible to vehicular traffic.

*Above:* Irish-born architect James Hoban's floor plan for the White House drew on the symmetry of 18th-century, Georgian-style architecture. Hoban won the top prize of $500 in an open design competition for the President's House held in 1792. *Left:* This stylized lithograph shows the north front of the White House in 1848, the same year Washington Monument work began, with figures in the foreground gathered across Pennsylvania Avenue. At the time, Pennsylvania Avenue was merely a dirt road; it would remain unpaved until after the Civil War.

In 1909, President William Howard Taft had a one-story office structure adjacent to the White House significantly expanded to provide more office space. It came to be called the West Wing and includes the Oval Office. On Christmas Eve 1929, an electrical fire broke out in the West Wing and caused significant damage. After it was rebuilt, the West Wing was expanded again during Franklin Roosevelt's tenure, as seen in this 1934 photograph. Roosevelt added a second floor, moved the Oval Office to its present location (which is adjacent to the Rose Garden), and installed a swimming pool so he could exercise his polio-stricken legs. President Nixon eventually turned the swimming pool into the Press Briefing Room, which also underwent a much-needed renovation in 2006.

Popular illustrator N. C. Wyeth produced this 1931 poster promoting Washington, D.C., tourism for the Pennsylvania Railroad.

## The White House Easter Egg Roll

The White House Easter Egg Roll, held on the Monday following Easter, is a long-standing Washington tradition, begun in 1878 when President Rutherford B. Hayes invited the children of government officials for games on the South Lawn. The Roll had previously been held on the Capitol grounds until some grumblers in Congress complained that the Capitol's lawn was not a playground and passed the Turf Protection Law, banning the practice. The Roll has been held at the White House every year, except during the two world wars and from 1946 to 1952, due to food-conservation initiatives and White House renovations. This black-and-white photograph from 1914 (*above*) shows children and their families participating in one of the last Rolls before America's entry into World War I. In 1941, the last White House Roll before the start of World War II, 53,000 children and their families showed up to chase eggs across the South Lawn, though typically, the crowd numbers slightly less than 20,000. Modern-day Rolls, such as the one in the photo to the right, feature storytellers, musical performers, lots of food, and, of course, a special appearance by the Easter Bunny.

*Above:* In its more than 200-year history, the White House, shown here today from the front, was variously known as the President's House, the Executive Mansion, and the President's Palace before Teddy Roosevelt dubbed it the White House in 1901. During his occupancy, Thomas Jefferson rigged a cistern and a system of wooden pipes into an early plumbing system. By the 1830s, the White House had hot and cold running water, which was a luxury at the time. In the 1840s, gas replaced candles and kerosene lamps until the house was wired for electricity in the 1890s. Television arrived in 1948 and the first computer by 1978. *Left:* President Obama meets with senior advisor David Axelrod (right) and two speechwriters in June 2009, in the Oval Office, which is situated in the West Wing.

# BLAIR HOUSE

Blair House is just across Pennsylvania Avenue from the White House and serves as a guesthouse for presidential visitors and other dignitaries. It's actually four 19th-century townhouses linked together to create a living space that, some would argue, is more elegant than the White House itself. With 119 rooms, including 35 bathrooms and a well-stocked flower shop, it does actually occupy more square footage.

The original home was built in 1824 for Dr. Joseph Lovell, first U.S. Surgeon General and organizer of the Army Corps of Engineers. In 1836, it was purchased by wealthy 19th-century publisher Francis Preston Blair Sr., who was a trusted advisor to populist president Andrew Jackson. The house eventually passed to his eldest son, Colonel Montgomery Blair, who served as postmaster general in the Lincoln administration and who, along with his father, was among those counseling Lincoln at the start of the Civil War. It was in Blair House that Robert E. Lee was offered—and declined—command of the Union army.

In 1942, Franklin Roosevelt arranged for the government to buy the Blair portion of the house for $175,000 in order to put up frequent wartime White House visitor Winston Churchill. First Lady Eleanor and the White House staff had finally had enough of Churchill's constant cigar smoking and his tendency to roam the executive mansion less than fully clothed.

A few years later, Harry Truman and his family took up official residence in Blair House while building engineers renovated the badly deteriorating White House. And in 1950, while Truman was inside, two Puerto Rican nationalists stormed the house in an attempt on the president's life. It was a scheme that took the lives of one of the would-be assassins and a guard.

President Harry Truman leaves Blair House for his newly acquired presidential duties at the White House in early May 1945, a little more than two weeks after the death of Franklin Roosevelt. Truman and his family stayed at Blair House during the transition period following Roosevelt's sudden death, then found themselves ensconced again in the official guesthouse in 1948, due to the near collapse of the White House. Architect Lorenzo S. Winslow and his team set to work, essentially gutting the White House and building out each room at a cost of $6 million. Ultimately, they corrected the shortcuts taken during the hasty rebuilding of the White House after it was torched during the War of 1812.

When a foreign emissary stays at Blair House, the presidential guesthouse flies the flag of that dignitary's country, signaling his or her presence. In April 2007, the Japanese flag flew in honor of the Japanese prime minister.

# THE U.S. TREASURY BUILDING

The U.S. Treasury Department was established in 1789, as Congress faced its first big governance task: financing the new nation and settling a $50 million Revolutionary War debt. For help, they turned to Alexander Hamilton, who, to his everlasting credit, pushed for a strong centralized bank instead of a system built on individual states' fractious interests. Hamilton's foresight resulted in credit worthiness so strong that it enabled Thomas Jefferson to negotiate the Louisiana Purchase in 1803, adding nearly a million square miles to the new nation's territory.

Hamilton, however, was no match for Aaron Burr. Burr was the vice president to Jefferson and was part of an early secessionist plot by the New England states. He challenged Hamilton to a duel in 1804; Hamilton was fatally wounded. Burr was later tried for treason, due to his attempt to gain personal control of the western territories. Remarkably, he was found not guilty.

Eleven secretaries followed Hamilton in the treasury post before the department finally received a permanent home. Today's Treasury Building was designed in 1833 by architect Robert Mills (who also designed the Washington Monument) and is featured on the back of the ten-dollar bill.

The U.S. Treasury Building, shown here today, is third among the city's oldest public buildings, following the White House and the Capitol. It was built in stages over 30 years, beginning in 1836 when Congress authorized construction of a guaranteed fireproof building after two earlier fires had destroyed this essential governmental department's headquarters. Until 1867, the State Department was housed in what eventually became the Treasury Building's North Wing before State was moved into the Old Executive Office Building. The statue shown is of Albert Gallatin, a Swiss-born financier elected from Pennsylvania to serve his district in the House. In 1801, Thomas Jefferson tapped Gallatin to serve as Secretary of the Treasury, a post he held until 1814, making Gallatin the longest serving secretary. The statue is the work of sculptor James Fraser, whose sculptures also grace the exterior of the Supreme Court Building.

# THE EISENHOWER EXECUTIVE OFFICE BUILDING

The Old Executive Office Building (or OEOB), shown here in the early 20th century, flanks the west side of the White House. Its ornate Second Empire style, with its mansard roof and elaborate facade, reflects late 19th-century tastes that were more European than American and contrasts sharply with the Greek Revival style of the Treasury Building, which borders the east side of the White House. When it was completed in 1888, the OEOB was the largest office building in Washington. It has seven levels, 553 rooms, eight curving granite staircases, and 83 working fireplaces.

Once headquarters of the War, State, and Navy departments, the Eisenhower Executive Office Building is one of the finest examples of the Second Empire style. Located just west of the White House, it is better known as the Old Executive Office Building. The designer, Alfred B. Mullet, was an English-born architect who was responsible for several important 19th-century American public buildings, including the San Francisco Mint.

Construction began in 1871, with the three departments gradually moving in over the next 17 years, which was how long it took to finish the job. By 1947, however, each department had outgrown its space and had moved to larger quarters. The building was then available for annexation by the White House, which was facing its own rapid executive expansion.

By the 1950s, the ornate behemoth that Harry Truman called "the greatest monstrosity in America" had fallen into such disrepair that it was scheduled for demolition. Fortunately, the wrecking ball was held off until 1969, when the building was declared a National Historic Landmark. In the 1980s, it was finally restored to its marble-tile, gold-leaf, and stained-glass glory.

Today, the south side of the Old Executive Office Building serves as backdrop to the Winged Victory First Army Division Monument. Dedicated in 1924, it was erected to honor the lives of members of the division who died during World War I. Cass Gilbert was the architect of the column featuring the Victory statue, which is the work of Daniel Chester French (perhaps best known for his statue of Abraham Lincoln seated inside the Lincoln Memorial).

The Willard Hotel was well along in its dotage and decline when this photo was taken in 1959 (*left*). In 1968, the landmark hotel closed, seemingly for good. Then the Pennsylvania Avenue Development Corporation, charged with revitalizing the avenue and adjacent downtown streets, bought the property and transferred ownership to a commercial developer. Unfortunately, though, the old hotel sat abandoned for the next 15 years. When the Willard finally reopened, it was fully restored. Its famous lobby, shown below in 2009, is still a favorite with powerbrokers and tourists alike.

# THE WILLARD HOTEL

One of a handful of original grand Washington hotels, the Willard has been in operation on its current site since 1850, when young hotelier Henry Willard and his brothers converted several row houses into a 100-room establishment. Senators, congressmen, diplomats, and presidents have stayed here, including Abraham Lincoln, who checked in while the White House was being readied for him. Later, in order to cover the bill, Lincoln had to sign over his entire first presidential paycheck—a little less than $775.

Another guest, New England abolitionist Julia Ward Howe, was visiting Washington with her husband not long after the Civil War began. She was so inspired by Union troops bivouacked nearby that, in her room one morning in 1861, she quickly penned the words to what would become "The Battle Hymn of the Republic."

Only two blocks from the White House, the Willard remained popular after the war, especially with office-seekers and others who came to Washington to press their cases. They would gather in the hotel's posh red-velvet lobby, hoping to catch President Grant, who favored the Willard's bar and restaurant. It was President Grant who began to refer to them as "lobbyists," a term that has since only stirred up stronger disapproval.

By the 1960s, the Willard had fallen into steep decline and was only spared demolition by a last-minute court order. After years of legal disputes and a costly makeover, the Willard reopened in 1986.

# IN AND AROUND LAFAYETTE SQUARE

In 1804, President's Park was formed when Thomas Jefferson cut Pennsylvania Avenue through parts of what were original White House grounds. Later, this area became known as Lafayette Square.

It was named for Marquis de Lafayette, a Revolutionary War hero and a major-general in Washington's Continental Army, who drew an adoring mob into the square on his last visit to the city in 1824. The grassy seven-acre public park is full of monuments to Revolutionary War heroes, including one to Lafayette himself, though the centerpiece is the statue of War of 1812 hero General Andrew Jackson on horseback—the first equestrian statue erected in the United States. Today, the park is mostly popular with lunchtime chess players and the mildly odd, who, by day, hoist their hand-painted signs espousing their various causes, as per their First Amendment rights, but who sadly and all too often spend their nights stretched out on the nearby heating grates.

In the 19th century, Lafayette Square was one of the city's most fashionable neighborhoods and included such elite as naval hero Stephen Decatur, who was the first to build a house there in 1818, and Dolley Madison, the vivacious and much-admired First Lady who moved to the Square in

1837 after her husband died. Her house was later owned by adventurer and South Pacific explorer Charles Wilkes, whose many specimens bolstered the Smithsonian's early collections.

By the beginning of the 20th century, plans called for demolition of many of the old homes in favor of a complex of government office buildings, a scheme that was fortunately trumped with development plans for Federal Triangle, a larger and much more accommodating site along Pennsylvania Avenue.

*Above:* Lafayette Square features a statue of Andrew Jackson on horseback, shown here today. The work of sculptor Clark Mills, it was erected in 1853 and cast from the brass guns Jackson captured in his victory over the British in Pensacola, Florida, and in New Orleans during the War of 1812. Jackson went on to be elected president in 1828. *Left:* Ambassador and entrepreneur General Edward F. Beale bought the Decatur House in 1872, installing parquet floors on the second floor, shown here today.

## The Church of the Presidents

Known as "The Church of the Presidents," St. John's Episcopal Church sits directly across Lafayette Square from the White House and has been attended by every president since 1816, when it held its first service. Pew 54 is reserved for the president's exclusive use. The church was designed by Benjamin Henry Latrobe, then the nation's premiere architect who also served as one of several early architects of the Capitol. The bell in St. John's steeple was cast in Boston by Paul Revere's son, Joseph, and has been in continuous use since it was installed in 1822.

## Lafayette Square's Grand Hotel

The Hay-Adams, directly opposite the White House across Lafayette Square, is one of the city's best hotels. It was named for two of the Square's most prominent citizens: John Milton Hay, assistant to President Abraham Lincoln, and Henry Brooks Adams, noted author and descendant of President John Adams, whose adjoining homes occupied this site. The two men and their wives, along with geologist Clarence King, were close friends and called themselves "The Five of Hearts." They hosted salons and posh parties that attracted such guests as Mark Twain, Theodore Roosevelt, and Henry James. After the Hays' and the Adams' deaths, Washington developer Harry Wardman, who built private homes across the city that are still prized for their quality, bought both homes in 1927; he razed them and built the Hay-Adams. The design is a mix of Italian Renaissance set off with classical Greek architectural elements, with touches of the Tudor and Elizabethan—the overall effect certainly makes today's Hay-Adams unique, as well as one of the city's most beautiful buildings.

## Washington's First Art Gallery

Today's red-brick Renwick Gallery (*left*) was the city's first art gallery, built in 1859 by architect James Renwick to house the collection of banker and philanthropist William Corcoran; it was originally known as the Corcoran Gallery. A sweeping red-carpeted staircase inside leads to the Victorian-style Grand Salon (*below*), where the paintings, stacked to the ceiling, include George Catlin's famous portraits of Native Americans. Early gallery-goers were scandalized when Corcoran put on display Hiram Powers's nude sculpture *The Greek Slave*—the custom at the time demanded that men and women view the statue separately. The sculpture, along with Corcoran's expanding collection, was long ago moved to the much larger Corcoran Gallery a few blocks away, where it remains shamelessly on display. By the 1960s, the Renwick, which had been converted into a government office building, was crumbling and ready to be torn down until First Lady Jacqueline Kennedy spearheaded a movement to save it. It has since been acquired by the Smithsonian Institution and is an extension of its National Museum of American Art.

In 1894, when this photo was taken, the Renwick Gallery was known as the Corcoran Gallery.

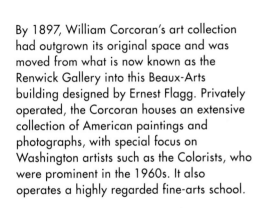

By 1897, William Corcoran's art collection had outgrown its original space and was moved from what is now known as the Renwick Gallery into this Beaux-Arts building designed by Ernest Flagg. Privately operated, the Corcoran houses an extensive collection of American paintings and photographs, with special focus on Washington artists such as the Colorists, who were prominent in the 1960s. It also operates a highly regarded fine-arts school.

## Octagon House

Once home to the prominent Tayloe family, the Octagon House was one of the few luxury homes in early 19th-century Washington and was designed by William Thornton, original architect of the Capitol. President James Madison and his wife, Dolley, lived here while the White House was being rebuilt after the British set it ablaze in August 1814. Built to accommodate an irregularly shaped lot, the Octagon House is an unusual mix of Georgian and Federal styles and, despite its name, actually has only six sides. It was home to the Tayloes until 1855 and then saw service successively as a school, a federal office building, and a boarding house. The American Institute of Architects eventually acquired the property and made it their headquarters in 1902.

One of many striking architectural features inside the Octagon House is this circular staircase, which, by a clever system of supports, appears to "float," as seen in this photograph.

This photo of the Daughters of the American Revolution headquarters, bottom left, and the headquarters of the American Red Cross, middle right, was taken in 1914. The two buildings, one dedicated to female descendants of those who served in the Revolution and the other to the memory of those women who served as nurses during the Civil War, are elegant additions to the 17th Street neighborhood.

## DAR Headquarters

The Daughters of the American Revolution have their headquarters here in Memorial Continental Hall, which features a museum devoted to American interior design as well as a library of genealogy. In 1929, the DAR built the adjacent Constitution Hall, designed by John Russell Pope, as a venue for their annual conventions. Its excellent acoustics, seating for 3,700, and convenient location just a few blocks from the White House soon made it the city's performance hall of choice. The DAR was founded in 1890 by a group of women descendants of Revolutionary War patriots, and today, it has more than 150,000 members.

# TAXATION WITHOUT REPRESENTATION: THE D.C. STATEHOOD DEBATE

The city's motto is *Justitia Omnibus*, which means "Justice for All"—all but the 600,000 citizens of Washington, D.C., that is. They have no voting representative in Congress, although they pay the full freight of federal taxes.

The founders established the capital city as part of a federal territory that also included the separate cities of Georgetown and Alexandria, with all of it under Congress's control. Alexandria was retroceded to Virginia in 1846. After the Civil War, Washington and Georgetown were combined to form the District of Columbia, which simplified administration but did nothing to extend the full rights of citizenship.

It wasn't until the ratification of the 23rd Amendment to the Constitution in 1961 that Washingtonians were finally able to vote in a presidential election. In 1973, Congress passed the Home Rule Act, which allowed the election of a mayor (the first was fittingly named Walter Washington) and a city council, although Congress retained strict oversight. Congress still has final say-so on any decisions the mayor and council make and keeps control of the purse strings. Although Congress has also permitted membership of one delegate to its ranks, it refuses to allow this delegate to cast a single vote on the House floor.

As a push against this injustice, a movement for D.C. statehood has slowly taken hold. Unlike Home Rule, statehood could not be repealed by Congress and would guarantee a vote. Opponents suggest that because Washington occupies land once owned by Maryland, the city should petition Maryland for readmittance in order to gain the vote.

A man on a ledge of the District Building, now called the Wilson Building, hoists a box of food while the man below fends it off with a broom. In March 1977, the building was taken over by 12 armed Hanafi Muslims. Others from their group also simultaneously stormed the Islamic Center on Massachusetts Avenue and the B'nai B'rith headquarters on Rhode Island Avenue. Altogether, they held about 150 hostages at the three sites for 39 hours, until police, working with the assistance of the ambassadors from Iran, Pakistan, and Egypt, finally persuaded the gunmen to surrender. It was the worst case of terrorism in the city's history until September 11, 2001.

# PENNSYLVANIA AVENUE

Famously known for that one-mile stretch between the White House and the Capitol, Pennsylvania Avenue is actually seven miles long, a puzzling road that starts in the west in Georgetown when M Street suddenly turns into the avenue at 29th Street. There, it winds confusingly around Washington Circle until it dead-ends at the Old Executive Office Building next to the White House. Since September 11, 2001, motorized traffic no longer passes here. Along the 1600 block, it's strictly a pedestrian mall now, though the White House can still be glimpsed through the iron fence. The area is patrolled by the Secret Service and capped by car-bomb deterring barriers that no amount of fancy pavers and pretty landscaping can disguise. It's a security zone, which means that the block once intended as the most preeminent of the "People's Capital" now has the distinct feel of a bunker.

Picking up the trail and heading east toward the Capitol, the avenue dead-ends again. It picks up once more through one of Washington's more troubled areas, crossing the Anacostia River over the Sousa Bridge, finally ending in a shaggy Maryland neighborhood. Planned as a grand avenue by Pierre L'Enfant in 1790 (perhaps he thought of the Champs-Élysées), it may have fallen a bit short of his dream.

Regardless, Pennsylvania Avenue is still prominent. Thomas Jefferson was the first to parade its length during his second inauguration in 1805, setting off the presidential tradition. Since then, it's become the route of choice for holiday revelers, funeral corteges, and marching protestors. But with no cohesive plan in place for either its development or maintenance, by the 1960s, America's so-called Main Street had turned into an eyesore. Therefore, in the 1970s, Congress established the Pennsylvania Avenue Development Corporation, which is charged with sprucing up what is indeed America's most famous avenue—a job that took until the turn of the 21st century to complete.

*Top:* Real elephants, not the Republican variety, came to town in this 1907 photograph of a Pennsylvania Avenue circus parade. *Bottom:* A drum and bugle corps stands at attention on Pennsylvania Avenue during a recent 4th of July parade. Long a popular route for parades of all sorts, including inaugurals, Pennsylvania Avenue's longest parade lasted for two days when, in May 1865, 200,000 troops marched in the Grand Review of the Union Armies.

# FEDERAL TRIANGLE

When construction on this federal office project began in the 1930s, it was the city's biggest expansion to date. The intention was to centralize the burgeoning federal government in a single location between the Capitol and the White House. The architects charged with the task designed each of the office buildings in a different style, resulting in a surprisingly harmonious mix that ranges from Greek Revival to art deco.

During the Depression years of the 1930s, when jobs were scarce, the Federal Triangle project employed hundreds of artisans and skilled laborers. The project also required leveling the remains of a notorious slum that had grown up during the Civil War. Known as Murder Bay, by 1900, practically every shack there was a brothel.

The Federal Triangle plan also called for the demolition of a Washington favorite, the Old Post Office, built in 1899. For 50 years, preservationists struggled to save it, winning their case in 1978 when restoration on the Old Post Office began. In the 1990s, Federal Triangle was completed with the opening of the Ronald Reagan Building and International Trade Center.

Today, the Federal Triangle buildings include the Commerce Department, the Interstate Commerce Commission, the Internal Revenue Service, the Justice Department, the Federal Trade Commission, the National Archives, and the Mellon Auditorium. The auditorium is part of the Treasury Department and is named for a former secretary.

The Old Post Office is a Romanesque Revival treasure that preservationists fought to save. Shown here in the 1920s, it was known fondly as "Old Tooth" for its denticulate tower. No longer a post office, today it contains shops, restaurants, and federal offices, including the National Endowment for the Humanities and the National Endowment for the Arts.

## Pennsylvania Avenue Slum

The neighborhood once known as Murder Bay, shown here in the 1860s, extended along the south side of Pennsylvania Avenue between the White House and the Capitol, and in the years following the Civil War, it became the city's worst slum. Freed slaves and poor whites crowded Murder Bay, living in hovels. Washington Canal, the city's most noxious waterway, flowed through the area, carrying diseases, such as malaria. Uneducated and mostly unemployed, residents of Murder Bay made their own economy, establishing gambling dens and houses of prostitution, the last of which weren't cleared until the 1930s, when construction on the massive Federal Triangle project began.

## Historic Watering Hole

Shown here in the late 19th century at its original Pennsylvania Avenue spot, Harvey's Restaurant was a Washington institution for more than 130 years. In 1862, owner George Harvey was credited with serving the first steamed oysters, mainly to satisfy impatient patrons unwilling to wait for the roasted version, which took longer to prepare. His saloon, which he'd opened in an old blacksmith's shop on the edge of Murder Bay, quickly became a restaurant serving 500 wagonloads of oysters a week. After two moves, Harvey's passed out of the family and closed its doors in 1991.

The Ronald Reagan Building and International Trade Center is a modern office complex that holds the offices of 7,000 federal employees as well as international trade consultants and nonprofit organizations. The building, named for the 40th president, was dedicated in 1998. Several important events have been held here, including celebrations for the 50th anniversary of the North Atlantic Treaty Organization (NATO). The amphitheater hosts a lunchtime schedule of performances and is home to the Capitol Steps, an amateur troupe of political satirists made up of congressional staffers with theatrical aspirations.

The elegant Mellon Auditorium is part of a three-building complex within Federal Triangle. It has been the scene of several important events, including the 2006 funeral for Philip Merrill (*right*), a prominent Washington magazine publisher and philanthropist. The auditorium was designed by Arthur Brown and was completed in 1934. It was named for Andrew Mellon, of the Pittsburgh banking family, who served as secretary of the treasury in the 1920s and was the financial force behind the establishment of the National Gallery of Art.

# THE NATIONAL ARCHIVES

The National Archives is a repository for all things American, from the Declaration of Independence, the Constitution, and the Bill of Rights to the Zapruder film, the Watergate tapes, and the White House documents leading up to the war in Iraq. The construction of the National Archives was a Depression-era Works Progress Administration project, and it not only created much-needed jobs, it was also responsible for centralizing the government's burgeoning records collection. Storing all sorts of national treasures, the Greek Revival-style building occupies the site of the old Center Market, a fulcrum of downtown commerce in the 19th century but long in decline by the time it was razed in 1931. As the government's files have continued to expand, so has the Archives' collection, which now incorporates several satellite locations and includes the various presidential libraries.

The original Declaration of Independence, seen here, as well as the Constitution and the Bill of Rights—known collectively as the Charters of Freedom—were first installed at the National Archives in 1952 and put on display in hermetically sealed cases.

The National Archives, shown here in 1943, is a neoclassical-style building designed by John Russell Pope. Completed in 1934, it features four large sculptures representing the Future, the Past, Heritage, and Guardianship, as well as several inscriptions cut in stone. It is the mission of the Archives to collect and catalogue the American past and to hold in trust for the public the documentary evidence of our national experience.

A shopper inspects goods for sale at Center Market on Pennsylvania Avenue in this photograph from the 1920s. When it opened in 1872, Center Market was one of the country's largest, with 1,000 indoor market stalls and parking space outside for 300 wagons, where farmers sold their produce directly to customers. From the city's beginning, there had always been a market here but never before was anything so grand. It was designed by Washington architect Adolph Cluss at the behest of Alexander "Boss" Shepherd, head of Public Works. The market was torn down in 1931 to make way for the National Archives building.

## Federal Bureau of Investigation

The FBI Building, opened in 1974, is known officially as the J. Edgar Hoover Building, named for the agency's infamous head who sat in uncontested control from 1924 until his death in 1972. Fittingly, it's an example of a school of architecture known as new brutalism. Bare bones and all angles, the style, which may have been meant to intimidate, is mostly just cold and off-putting, making FBI headquarters one of Washington's least attractive buildings.

## All About the News

Lest anyone forget it, the Newseum on Pennsylvania Avenue, devoted to all things journalistic, is here to remind us that freedom of speech, particularly of the press, is guaranteed in the United States. The words of the First Amendment are engraved on a 74-foot granite slab on the side of the building, so that every member of Congress can clearly see them from the Capitol, just a few blocks away. Opened in 2008, the Newseum contains 250,000 square feet of exhibit space. Perhaps its most moving exhibit is the gallery of photographs shot by Pulitizer Prize winners, who have photographed everything from wars to daring rescues to family pets and babes in arms. Outside, street-level interactive screens keep passersby abreast of the news from around the world.

German Vice Chancellor and Minister of Foreign Affairs Frank Walter Steinmeier pauses before a section of the Berlin Wall, which is a part of an exhibit at the Newseum. The Berlin Wall was erected in 1961, part of the post–World War II partition of Germany into the Soviet-controlled east and the free west, which marked the beginning of the so-called Cold War. For the best part of three decades, East Berliners did their best to escape over, under, or around the wall, while on the west side, graffiti artists expressed their sentiments about their divided city with spray paint. The side of the wall that faced East Berlin, opposite the side shown here, is completely blank. The wall was finally torn down in 1989.

## Canadian Embassy

In 1989, Canada opened its new embassy on Pennsylvania Avenue. It's the only country with an official presence within easy walking distance of both the Capitol and the White House. This modern wedge-shape building occupies the former site of a 19th-century boarding house and was designed by Arthur Erickson, Canada's most forward-thinking architect. He incorporated elements of his native country into the interior of the building's design. Thanks to the embassy's location, friends and guests of the ambassador enjoy front row seats to the city's premiere events, especially the 4th of July parades and the Presidential Inaugural parades along Pennsylvania Avenue, which they can enjoy from the glass-enclosed balcony.

The Canadian embassy features a grand rotunda supported by 12 columns, one for each of the country's ten provinces and its two territories at the time the embassy was constructed. Another territory was added to the nation in 1999. The rotunda is surrounded by a waterfall that symbolizes Niagara Falls, which straddles the Canadian-U.S. border.

Architect Benjamin Latrobe substantially modified the Capitol building's design by original architect William Thornton, expanding the Senate chamber and constructing a new chamber for the House. Latrobe resigned his post in 1817 and was replaced by Charles Bulfinch, who added the Capitol's signature dome. The dome, in this lithograph from 1825, is the Capitol's first and was replaced with a much larger dome when the Capitol was expanded in the 1850s.

# THE U.S. CAPITOL

City planner Pierre L'Enfant envisioned the Capitol, the true home of the republic, as the geographic center of the city and the point from which its quadrants are marked. Dr. William Thornton, a physician from the Virgin Islands, designed the Capitol. Thornton had no architectural training but nonetheless impressed George Washington with his grand but simple plan. During construction, however, Thornton clashed with the building supervisors—one of them actually *was* an architect and was quite resentful of the doctor. Construction somehow stumbled along, and by November 1800, Congress met for the first time in the completed Senate chamber.

Benjamin Henry Latrobe eventually replaced Thornton. Latrobe was a Pennsylvanian and America's best-known architect; he tackled the construction of the House. By 1811, the Capitol was more or less complete, but unfortunately, the British torched it during the War of 1812. Latrobe bent to the task of rebuilding but was soon drawn by other more lucrative projects—those that didn't require dealing with the egos of congressmen. Mild-mannered New Englander Charles Bulfinch then replaced Latrobe; it was Bulfinch who linked the two chambers and erected the all-important dome.

By the time 1850 rolled around, there were more states in the union, and Congress had outgrown its lodgings. It ordered a Capitol expansion, which naturally required a bigger dome. For this they turned to Thomas U. Walter, who cleverly overlaid two cast-iron shells and painted them to look like marble, which is the dome seen today. Finally, installed in 1863 was Thomas Crawford's famous bronze statue: the robed woman with sword, laurel wreath, and shield, known as the Statue of Freedom.

Before gathering in its present chamber, the Senate met in this room in the Capitol that architect Benjamin Latrobe designed (*below*). For 40 years, the Senate met under the domed ceiling, debating the issue of slavery that defined so much of America during the first half of the 19th century. The red velvet-swagged platform in the center is the desk of the vice president, who also serves as President of the Senate. When the Senate moved in 1859, the Supreme Court, which had its chambers directly below, took the Senate's place.

## Statuary Hall

The House of Representatives met in this domed and marble room (*above*) until 1857, when it moved to its present and significantly larger chamber. Stately and grand as it seems, this room has one major flaw: Its shape and the materials on its surfaces combine to make a distinctive echo, which, when it served as the House's chamber, allowed opposing parties to eavesdrop rather easily on each other's conversations. After the House moved, the old chamber found new purpose as Statuary Hall and was rededicated in 1864. Here, each state puts on display statues of two of its most prominent citizens, which include everyone from Louisiana's populist Huey Long to Utah's Mormon leader Brigham Young.

This contemporary view of the U.S. Capitol Building shows the west front. When Congress first met in the Capitol in 1800, there were only 30 senators and 106 representatives, but by 1850, membership had more than doubled, which meant expansion was necessary. Architect Thomas U. Walter set to work, replacing the original Virginia sandstone used to construct the Capitol with better-grade marble from Massachusetts and Maryland. By 1859, both wings were complete, and the basic footprint of the building was in place as it stands today. But the expanded building dwarfed Bulfinch's original dome, which Walter replaced with this much larger cast-iron version, inspired by the domes of St. Peter's in Rome and St. Paul's in London.

## Freedom

In 1854, Congress commissioned Thomas Crawford to sculpt a statue for the top of the Capitol dome. *Freedom,* as the bronze is called, is an allegorical female figure holding a sword, a laurel wreath, and a shield with 13 stripes, one for each of the colonies. Her helmet features an eagle's head with feathers and is encircled with stars. It was hoisted atop the Capitol dome in 1863, and except during its restoration in the 1990s, it has been in place there ever since.

The plaster mold used to cast *Freedom* languished for decades in various government building basements. In 2009, it was installed in the new U.S. Capitol Visitor Center.

*Brumidi's Rotunda*

The centerpiece of the Capitol is its rotunda, a grand ceremonial space under the Capitol dome where presidents, legislators, and military heroes have lain in state. Presiding over all has been Constantino Brumidi's *Apotheosis of Washington,* the fresco seen here featuring George Washington surrounded by several allegorical figures, most prominently Liberty, Victory, and Fame. Brumidi, classically trained in his native Italy, arrived in the United States in 1852 as the Capitol was undergoing expansion. Montgomery Meigs, engineer in charge of the project, tapped Brumidi to decorate the Capitol's interior. And decorate he did. Brumidi, a master of *buon fresco,* in which the artist paints directly onto wet mortar, worked for 25 years on the Capitol. He covered not only the Rotunda but also entire rooms and corridors with his lavish and detailed designs.

## QUAD CITY

To those unfamiliar with its layout, Washington, D.C.'s famous circles, diagonals, squares, and quadrants can make getting around a bewildering experience. There is, however, a system to what appears to be madness. Washington is divided into four quadrants—Northwest, Northeast, Southwest, and Southeast—with each quadrant running in a compass direction from the U.S. Capitol according to city planner Pierre L'Enfant's original scheme. Within the quadrants, numbered streets run north to south; lettered streets, east to west. Now come the avenues, which are named for the states and run diagonally, cutting across the street grid and intersecting other avenues to form the circles, such as Dupont Circle and Washington Circle. Where the avenues meet numbered streets, they form the squares, such as Lafayette Square and Mount Vernon Square. Most addresses officially include a quadrant designation, and it's easy to see why. The M Street that runs through the center of popular Georgetown is in Northwest and is not the same M Street adjacent to the waterfront. That M Street is in Southwest. And while the Library of Congress and the Supreme Court are next-door neighbors on First Street, they're in two different quadrants: the library in Southeast, the high court in Northeast. Checking a map will show East, North, and South Capitol streets, but no West Capitol Street. That was replaced by the Mall, which runs between the Capitol and the Potomac and is home to many of the Smithsonian museums. There's also no J Street, due to the similarity between the letters "J" and "I" in the script style of the 19th century. There are, however, four "I" streets, sometimes written "Eye" for clarity. The letters X, Y, Z, and B are also absent from the grid; the exclusion of X, Y, and Z is unexplained. As for B, there were once two of them, straddling the north and south sides of the Mall. They've since been renamed Independence and Constitution avenues.

This early 20th-century photograph shows the Bartholdi Fountain, designed by Frederic-Auguste Bartholdi of Statue of Liberty fame. It is the centerpiece of a small park adjacent to the Botanic Garden.

Lush flowers line a pool at the United States Botanic Garden at the foot of Capitol Hill. The garden was originally established as a kind of holding tank after the congressionally mandated 1842 Wilkes Expedition, led by the explorer Charles Wilkes, returned after four years traveling the globe with more than 50,000 plant specimens. Wilkes and his crew also brought back 4,000 animals and insects along with thousands of gems and fossils. The collection formed what would eventually become the Smithsonian Institution and the Botanic Garden. Today, the Botanic Garden holds approximately 26,000 plants, with its orchid collection as the highlight.

# THE U.S. SUPREME COURT

Early on, the executive and legislative branches of government each had fixed locations, but the the judicial branch remarkably had no permanent home in Washington until 1935.

In 1928, William Howard Taft (the only president to have also served on the court) was successful in convincing Congress to allocate funds for a building. It was designed by architect Cass Gilbert and was built on the former site of the Old Capitol Prison, where celebrated Confederate spy Belle Boyd had once been held.

The Court first met in 1790 in the Merchants Exchange Building in New York and then, when the government moved to Washington, in a succession of private homes, taverns, and hotels—for a time it even met in the Capitol building itself. It handed down its first important decision in 1803 in the case of *Marbury v. Madison,* which determined the Court's right to uphold or strike down laws based on their constitutionality. Its decision in the Dred Scott case in 1857 declared that slaves were not persons and therefore not entitled to equal protection under the law. By 1954, however, it had ruled in favor of Linda Brown in the famous case against the Board of Education of Topeka, Kansas, which ended school segregation. Its 1966 decision in *Miranda v. Arizona* guaranteed suspects in an arrest access to their legal rights, and its 1973 decision in *Roe v. Wade* effectively guaranteed the right to abortion. In 2000, it decided the outcome of the presidental election when it ruled in favor of the constitutionality of the Electoral College.

For years, the U.S. Supreme Court—the smallest branch of the federal government, with only nine members plus staff—met in a variety of makeshift locations, its longest tenure in rooms inside the Capitol. Finally, in 1935, it moved into this classical marble masterpiece designed by Cass Gilbert, prominent in the Beaux-Arts movement. The broad staircase is flanked by two works by American sculptor James Fraser, *Contemplation of Justice* and *Authority of Law.* And carved into the pediment above the entrance are those immortal words: "Equal Justice Under Law."

# THE LIBRARY OF CONGRESS

The Library of Congress, a Beaux-Arts beauty, opened in 1897—it may be the most spectacular building in Washington. The library's collection comes to more than 200 million books, rare manuscripts, maps, photographs, recordings, films, and more. Its treasures include a Gutenberg Bible, a draft of Jefferson's Declaration of Independence, an early Thomas Edison film, and the world's largest collection of comic books.

The original library was located in the Capitol Building and was intended for legislators only. After the Capitol was torched by the British in the War of 1812, Thomas Jefferson (who needed the money) sold his own 6,500-volume library to Congress (which needed the books) for $24,000, thus reestablishing the library.

Interestingly enough, yet another fire in the Capitol (this one in 1851, owing to a faulty fireplace) destroyed much of that collection and left what remained in such disarray that it was all but useless as a resource. So, Congress allotted money for the rebuilding of today's library, known as the Jefferson Building. It was built on a block of buildings called Carroll Row, which included a slave market, the boarding house where Lincoln lived when he was a congressman, and the upscale Long's Hotel, which was the site of James Madison's inaugural ball.

The library, in order to increase its holdings, eventually (and wisely) opened its doors to the public. But it soon outgrew its space. Two adjunct buildings opened on Capitol Hill to handle the overflow: the John Adams Building in 1939 and the James Madison Building in 1981. The three buildings combined have 500 miles of shelf space, but even that isn't enough. The library also operates several warehouses and storage facilities that are scattered across the metro area.

This photo shows artisans at work on the sculptures for the Library of Congress in 1894. The architectural plans were drawn up by the firm of Smithmeyer & Pelz of Washington, D.C., and Congress approved the plans in 1886. Construction went in fits and starts until the building was finally completed in 1897. The Library came in $200,000 under budget, costing a little more than $6 million.

Every day, as they ascend the staircase into the Library of Congress's main Jefferson Building, thousands enjoy American sculptor Roland Hinton Perry's *Court of Neptune Fountain*, which features Neptune, Roman god of the sea; Triton, his son; and several water nymphs.

## The Library of Congress, Jefferson Building

When the Jefferson Building of the Library of Congress was completed in 1897, it was proclaimed the most beautiful building in Washington (*right*). Some argue that it still is. Exterior adornments to this block-long colossus include carvings of 33 heads of various ethnic groups, from Arab to Zulu, set in the keystones of the first-floor windows, and the busts of Emerson, Goethe, Franklin, Dante, Hawthorne, and other notables across the front portico. Just inside the front entrance, the Great Hall (*below*), all gilt and marble with stained-glass skylights, rises 75 feet to the ceiling, its leitmotif fittingly inspired by Minerva, the Roman goddess of wisdom (and sister of Neptune). The Hall and its corridors and rooms were once partitioned and used as office space. The mosaics and murals in the vaulted ceilings, the plaster medallions, and the marble columns were left uncared for and crumbling until Congress approved $81 million for restoration. In 1997, on its 100th anniversary, the Jefferson Building was reopened after an extensive renovation, and the Great Hall's grand spaces are now used to exhibit the library's many treasures.

# FOLGER SHAKESPEARE LIBRARY

The Folger opened in 1932 after oil mogul Henry C. Folger bought several Capitol Hill townhouses at distressed prices and converted them into space for his world-renowned Shakespeare collection. (He died before he could see the finished product.) Today, the Folger is home to the world's largest collection of Shakespeare's printed works, including his First Folios, dating from 1623. It also contains a replica of the Globe Theater, which offers a regular schedule of performances. Also, since 1980, the Washington branch of PEN, a writers' organization, has awarded the prestigious PEN/Faulkner Award in a ceremony held in the banquet room. Past winners have included John Updike, E. L. Doctorow, and Michael Cunningham.

*Above:* The Folger's Elizabethan Theatre offers timeless and modern adaptations of the bard's work. The theatre, with its wooden balconies and oak columns, is reminiscent of the theatres of Shakespeare's day, when traveling theatrical troupes played to audiences gathered in the courtyards and along the balconies of inns. The theatre also hosts lectures and readings, along with the Folger Consort, Washington's much-loved early music ensemble. *Left:* The Folger's Old Reading Room is outfitted with oak paneling and includes a large fireplace and French and Flemish tapestries. The ashes of founder Henry Folger and his wife, Emily, are interred in this room that is devoted to scholarly research; it is opened to the public only once each year, for Shakespeare's birthday celebration in April. The Folger has more than 300,000 books; 50,000 paintings and engravings; and other holdings including playbills, costumes, and musical instruments.

## Early Feminists' Headquarters

The Sewall-Belmont House became headquarters for the National Woman's Party in 1929. Its library, shown above in 1943, was named in honor of Florence Bayard Hilles, an early president of the party, and it grew to hold more than 3,000 volumes, plus photographs, diaries, letters, banners, and other artifacts from the early suffragist movement. But by the 1970s, with the modern-day feminist movement making enormous strides in the improvement of women's lives, the library seemed anachronistic and fell into disuse. Renewed interest in the collection in the 1990s led to the restoration of the library, which is once again open to the public.

## Capitol Hill's Eastern Market

*Above:* Vendors ply their wares outside Eastern Market in 1889. Opened in 1873, when the city had several such establishments, Eastern Market was built as part of the post–Civil War Public Works program that brought much-needed infrastructure and other improvements. By the early 20th century, this fresh-food emporium had become the fulcrum of Capitol Hill life and was significantly expanded to meet demand. But by the 1930s, the market had become the target of modern commercial development and was suffering from competition with the increasingly popular grocery chains. Preservationists, however, prevailed, banding together to save Eastern Market and making it a Capitol Hill mainstay. *Right:* Customers browse Eastern Market in August 2009 during its grand reopening. Fire tore through the block-long market in 2007, destroying much of the building and forcing vendors to put up in an adjacent schoolyard until the $22-million restoration project could be completed. The new Eastern Market has retained its original flavor, selling fresh fruits and vegetables, cheeses, fish, meats, and flowers. On Saturdays, artisans, crafters, antique dealers, and collectors gather in a kind of flea market, setting up their stalls around the exterior of the building.

# UNION STATION

In its early days, the city staked its commercial success on the Potomac and the C & O Canal until the railroads made the iron horse king. And by the late 19th century, the competing Pennsylvania and B&O railroads had turned the Mall into a tangle of unsightly tracks. Enter master architect Daniel Burnham, best known for his work on Chicago's 1893 World Columbian Exposition. He proposed a single grand building where all the railroad lines would converge.

"Make no little plans" was Burnham's credo, and when applied to the Union Station project, the result was a structure inspired by the Baths of Roman Emperor Diocletian. Erected on the edge of an immigrant neighborhood known, improbably, as Swampoodle, Union Station overwhelmed Capitol Hill when it opened in 1907. Composed of gold leaf, with Constantinian arches and classical statues by Louis Saint-Gaudens, the concourse at the majestic Union Station was the world's largest hall.

In the 1920s, 300 trains arrived at Union Station every day. By World War II, the terminal was thick with deploying servicemen, and the so-called "government girls," who had arrived to take up federal employment. Even Washington residents with no travel plans came to enjoy a meal at the station's elegant Savarin restaurant.

But by the 1960s, when train travel dropped, Union Station fell into disrepair. A badly executed plan to remake the abandoned station into a National Visitors Center failed in the 1970s. Finally, in 1981, private and public investors, fueled by a preservationist spirit, put up close to $200 million for a rescue job that took 200 artisans eight years to complete. Every year, 32 million travelers pass through the restored Union Station, which is now a prized landmark.

*Above:* A lithograph of Union Station, Washington, D.C., dated 1906. *Left:* The Columbus Fountain at Columbus Circle has marked the entrance to Union Station, Washington's grand train terminal, since 1912. Sculptor Lorado Taft's explorer stands between figures depicting the Old World, on the right, and the New World, on the left. Taft was a prominent Chicago sculptor, active in the Beaux-Arts movement and associated with architect Daniel Burnham, who designed Union Station.

Union Station's Great Hall is shown here in 1942 (*right*). At one time, Union Station employed as many as 5,000 people, who were there to man the liquor store, bowling alley, butcher shop, Turkish bath, YMCA, police station, and even the mortuary that operated inside the station. Presidents and visiting dignitaries often stayed at the station's exclusive Presidential Suite, which is now B. Smith's, one of Washington's most elegant restaurants. But by the middle of the century, train travel was declining, and its Washington demise was illustrated rather dramatically one January morning in 1953: The Pennsylvania Railroad's Federal Express, carrying passengers for President Dwight D. Eisenhower's inaugural along Track 16, slammed into Union Station at full speed. The 1,200 tons of runaway train crashed through the concourse floor. Amazingly, no one was killed, though the disaster signaled the beginning of the end for Union Station—or so it seemed.

Today, the Great Hall has undergone an extensive renovation (*left*). With passage in Congress of the Redevelopment Act of 1981, funds were made available that enabled the government to partner with private developers, and the transformation of the leaky old Union Station began. When they started, workers discovered the marbled halls had been turned into rookeries. There was trash everywhere, the floors had buckled, the ceilings had collapsed, and there were even a few squatters. The new Union Station was finally unveiled after eight years of painstaking work, with a gala to celebrate the reopening that drew a crowd of 3,000 to a sumptuous supper in the Great Hall. Today, in addition to Amtrak train service, Union Station has dozens of shops, several restaurants, and a multiplex movie theater.

## Monuments, Museums, and the Mall

# The National Mall: America's Front Yard

Every year, 25 million visitors come to the Mall: the two-mile-long, grassy expanse that stretches from the foot of the Capitol to the Potomac River, lined with museums and filled with the city's most inspiring monuments and memorials. By far, the Mall's two most popular stops are the Smithsonian's Air and Space Museum, which houses everything from biplanes to spaceships, and the Vietnam War Memorial, which consists of polished black granite slabs that are set below grade and engraved with the names of the fallen. Also, across Memorial Bridge, erected in remembrance of the Civil War's dead, lies stately Arlington Cemetery, once the Virginia plantation home of Robert E. Lee and now the final resting place for more than 300,000 who served their country.

### MULTIFUNCTIONAL MALL

The Mall was intended—according to Pierre L'Enfant's original 1791 city plan—as a grand public space; however, it wasn't until 1851 that a landscape architect, Andrew Jackson Downing, was actually commissioned to draw up a detailed design. Downing, unfortunately, died in a steamboat explosion before his plan could be executed, leaving the Mall to languish until early in the 20th century. Part cow pasture, part slum, America's Front Yard (as it's known) was also crisscrossed with the unsightly tracks of several railroad lines. The Washington Monument—begun in 1848 and finally completed 40 years later—and the Castle—the Smithsonian's original museum, which opened in 1855—were the Mall's only attractions. In 1901, a commission headed by James McMillan, a senator from Michigan, set about to change all that. The Mall was cleared, the train lines were relocated to the new Union Station on Capitol Hill, and land was set aside for the Lincoln Memorial.

*Opposite:* Protestors crowd Pennsylvania Avenue as they advance toward the Capitol during a rally to end the Vietnam War on April 26, 1971. This demonstration, one of several planned for that spring, drew about 200,000.

American casualties of the Spanish-American War await burial at Arlington National Cemetery in 1898. The war began with the sinking of the USS *Maine* in Havana harbor in Cuba in February of that year. Nearly 3,600 Americans died in the conflict, many of them from disease.

But as America entered the new century and geared for war, the expanding government claimed the Mall as the perfect spot to erect office buildings and living quarters, which were intended to be temporary. These ugly "tempos," as they were known, persisted well past the end of World War II, when, as the expanding Smithsonian demanded more space, they were gradually pulled down.

## CELEBRATIONS AND PROTESTS

The Mall is also America's best-known staging ground. As the site of the annual 4th of July celebration, it draws tens of thousands for a free concert and fireworks display, and the Smithsonian's popular summer Folk Life Festival, which celebrates the world's customs and cultures, is also held here. In 1894, when the country was in the midst of an economic depression, a small group of unemployed people—called Coxey's Army, for the Ohio businessman who led them—marched on the Mall seeking relief from Congress, only to be beaten and arrested in a demonstration of hard-heartedness that marked the divide between the haves and have-nots during the Gilded Age. Members of the National Woman's Party, an early suffragist group, marched here on Woodrow Wilson's inauguration day in 1913, attempting—but mostly failing—to draw his attention to their cause. In 1932, the Bonus Army, a group of World War I veterans who had been paid a pittance while war workers at home had earned high wages, camped on the Mall, after unsuccessfully pressing their case in Congress for back pay. The Mall also served as command central for some of the most important events of the 1960s, most notably Martin Luther King Jr.'s "I Have a Dream" speech and the antiwar movement that drew thousands of student protestors during the Vietnam War. More recently, on January 20, 2009, in weather just below freezing, two million people—the single largest gathering ever on the Mall—huddled to witness Barack Obama take the oath of office to become the 44th President of the United States.

## THE SLAVE TRADE

While the miserable vestiges of the slave trade have all but vanished from the nation's capital, many who know Washington and witnessed the swearing in of the country's first African American president must have noted that he took the oath of office not far from the city's most notorious former slave markets. As part of the Compromise of 1850—a mess of provisos that attempted to settle the slavery issue in the new territories—the slave trade was outlawed in Washington, but slave ownership itself remained legal. In the mid-19th century, there were around 3,000 slaves in Washington. It was an amount that was considerably less than the estimated 500,000 slaves in Maryland and Virginia, but Washington's Potomac River location allowed easy shipment of slaves south and made it the center of a brisk trade. One of the worst slave markets was the Yellow House, where humans were herded and kept in underground pens within sight and sound of the Capitol. "The voices of patriotic representatives boasting of freedom and equality, and the rattling of the poor slave's chains, almost commingled," wrote

The Vietnam Veterans Memorial lists the names of those Americans killed in the Vietnam War.

Solomon Northrup, a free black man from New York who had been kidnapped and sold into slavery in Washington. Chillingly, the Saint Charles Hotel, which was another slave market on the "worst" list and was probably the closest to the Capitol, wasn't even torn down until 1924—nearly 60 years after the end of the Civil War.

## COMING OF A NEW AGE

More than a little bedraggled after years of wear and tear, today, the Mall is due for a sprucing up, though Congress is reluctant to spring for the estimated $50 million required merely to replenish the lawns, tend to the trees, and install much-needed restroom facilities—never mind making more extensive improvements. But the Trust for the National Mall, a private citizens' group, has banded together with the National Park Service, which manages the Mall and most of Washington's other green spaces, to raise the necessary funds. It maintains that it is not only a matter of preserving the Mall's treasures, but it is vital to the nation's spirit that the Mall be preserved and revered "as a public space for democratic expression."

The Atlantic and Pacific arches of the World War II Memorial (foreground) flank a pool; between the arches is the curved Freedom Wall, marked with 4,000 gold stars in honor of the 400,000 fallen during the war. The long Reflecting Pool leads from the World War II Memorial to the Lincoln Memorial.

# THE MALL AND THE SMITHSONIAN INSTITUTION

City planner Pierre L'Enfant might have envisioned the Mall—the swath of green between the Capitol and the Potomac—lined with private residences and quality shops, but what it's become is better still: the Smithsonian's prime address.

The Smithsonian Institution is named for James Smithson, a British scientist. When he died in 1829, he left his inheritance to Congress with the stipulation that it establish an institution for research and scholarship in his name. Joseph Henry, a physicist from Princeton, was appointed as its first secretary. Charles Wilkes embarked on a four-year journey to explore the

Pacific at Congress's behest, and by 1842, he returned with thousands of rare items for the Smithsonian, including gems, tropical plants, and cultural artifacts from the oceanic peoples. In 1855, the Smithsonian opened its first building. Called the Castle, it is a Normanesque red sandstone structure designed by James Renwick, who also designed the city's first art gallery near the White House.

Since then, the Smithsonian hasn't stopped collecting; it boasts more than 130 million items. Of its 19 museums and nine research centers— the National Zoo is also under its province—

11 of its museums are on the Mall. They include, among others, the Freer and Sackler Galleries, which specialize in Asian collections; the National Museum of African Art; and the National Museum of the American Indian.

Unfortunately, the Smithsonian, lovingly known as "The Nation's Attic," has succumbed in recent years to fiscal malfeasance and facility neglect. In 2007, the situation was so bad that Secretary Lawrence Small, a former banker, was forced out and replaced by former Georgia Tech president Wayne Clough, whose amiable but scholarly style is slowly restoring the institution's luster.

The Mall has often been referred to as "America's Front Yard." But for several decades during the 20th century, in order to meet the increasing demand for government office space, it was crammed with government "tempo" buildings, such as these, still under construction in 1942. These bare-bones, two-story rectangles, some of which also served as dormitories for housing defense workers on the home front, were first built during World War I and were intended to be torn down once the crisis had passed, but by World War II, Washington's office and housing shortage had only increased. In the 1950s and '60s, the "tempos" were slowly torn down, though a few of these eyesores were still standing well into the 1970s.

First-line protestors clasp hands during an anti–Vietnam War rally held on the Mall in October 1967. This was the city's first anti-war rally of any size. Other historic gatherings on the Mall have been less divisive, such as the Million Man March, held in 1995, in which black men rallied in support of their families, neighborhoods, businesses, and themselves.

An 1848 bill of sale from one of the many slave markets present in Washington, D.C., at the time

Barack Obama was sworn in as the 44th President of the United States on January 20, 2009, at the U.S. Capitol, West Front, seen in the distance. An estimated two million spectators gathered that freezing day to watch the historic event—more than have ever been on the Mall at one time. Until Ronald Reagan had it moved to the West Front, the inaugural was typically held on the East Front, which faces the Supreme Court and the Library of Congress, but which doesn't offer the space to accommodate a crowd of any size.

The Smithsonian Institution was originally housed in this red-brick, Normanesque building, seen here in a photograph from 1870. "The Castle," as it's known, was built by James Renwick in 1855 and also served as the residence for Joseph Henry, the Smithsonian's first secretary. The crypt of James Smithson, for whom the Smithsonian is named, is located in the Castle, which today serves primarily as the information center for visitors to all the Smithsonian's museums.

## JAMES SMITHSON AND HIS GIFT TO THE NATION

AMERICA'S BEST-KNOWN COMPLEX of art and history museums—and one of Washington's main attractions—the Smithsonian Institution owes its existence to an Englishman, James Smithson, who never even set foot on these shores. James Smithson, originally christened James Lewis Macie, was born out of wedlock in 1765 to Elizabeth Keate Macie and Hugh Percy, a newly ennobled duke. In 1800, Smithson, who by then had distinguished himself at Oxford in his scientific studies, inherited his mother's fortune and then legally adopted his father's actual surname. Shunned by the English aristocracy because of the circumstances of his birth, Smithson left his entire estate, roughly $500,000, to the United States when he died in 1829, with instructions that an institution for the advancement of knowledge be founded in his name. Smithson's relations contested the will, and the legal battle lasted nine years before the money was finally deposited in the Philadelphia Mint. Then it took Congress eight years to figure out how to use Smithson's generous gift. Finally, in 1846, President James Polk signed the bill establishing the Smithsonian Institution. Joseph Henry, a physicist from Princeton, served as the first secretary, putting the institution's emphasis on scientific research. Its second secretary, Spencer Fullerton Baird, rather astutely shifted the focus to the institution's collections. Today, the Smithsonian is the world's largest museum complex, with holdings that exceed 136 million objects displayed in 19 museums, with plans for more museums on the way.

One of the most popular exhibits at the Smithsonian's National Museum of American History is The Gown Gallery, which features gowns worn by First Ladies Jacqueline Kennedy, Mamie Eisenhower, and Eleanor Roosevelt (*left to right*). The museum's collection began with a mix of gadgets and inventions originally held at the U.S. Patent Office, then combined with leftovers from the 1876 Centennial Exposition in Philadelphia. Today, the Museum of American History holds more than 3 million objects, including Lincoln's top hat and a Woodstock poster.

A 2,300-pound, 45-foot full-scale model of a North Atlantic right whale named Phoenix dominates the atrium in the new Sant Ocean Hall at the Smithsonian's National Museum of Natural History. Ocean Hall opened in 2008 and is named for benefactors Victoria and Roger Sant. At 23,000 square feet, it's the museum's largest exhibit, intended to focus attention on the importance and imperiled health of our oceans. Opened in 1910, the Natural History Museum is devoted to all things natural and includes exhibits on dinosaurs, fossils, Ice Age mammals, plants, insects, and minerals and gems, with its most precious specimen the famous Hope Diamond.

*The National Museum of the American Indian*

The Smithsonian's National Museum of the American Indian opened in 2004, its curvy limestone exterior an impressionistic reflection of the American West's wind- and water-carved landscape. Inside, the museum's centerpiece is its Potomac rotunda, which soars to 120 feet and serves as a staging ground for native dancing, craft demonstrations, and ceremonial performances. There are more than 800,000 artifacts of indigenous peoples displayed on five floors, everything from feather bonnets and weavings to totem poles, works in silver and gold, beading, ivory carvings, and hunting implements.

# THE NATIONAL GALLERY OF ART

From an architectural standpoint, the two buildings comprising the National Gallery of Art—on the Mall but not part of the Smithsonian—are strikingly different. The West Building, designed by John Russell Pope, is all neo-classical gracefulness and balance; the East Building, designed by I. M. Pei, is all modern angles that were designed to fit its trapezoidal-shape lot. Combined, the two house one of the world's best collections, charting the progression of art from the Middle Ages to the 21st century.

The West Building opened in 1941 on the former site of the B&O railroad terminal, one of several cluttering the Mall before the tracks were moved to Union Station. On July 2, 1881, while boarding a train at this station, Charles Guiteau, a disgruntled office seeker, shot President James Garfield. Garfield died three months later, and Guiteau was hanged for his crime. This building was seeded with the collection amassed by Andrew Mellon, who was of the Mellon banking family and was once a Treasury Secretary. His intention was to establish a world-class art museum in the nation's capital and to encourage the nation's wealthy to contribute their collections as well. And they did—to the point that the gallery required another building, the East Building, which opened in 1978. The East Building now occupies part of a neighborhood once known unflatteringly as Hash Row, for all the boarding houses crammed into its blocks.

The federal government funds the National Gallery's operations, but all the art it contains—from early Italian altarpieces to examples of American abstract expressionism—has been privately donated.

*Above:* Andrew W. Mellon began collecting art in the 1920s and encouraged fellow members of the affluent class to do likewise. In 1937, he authorized, with Congress's blessing and his cash, the building of this neo-classically styled gallery (known today as the West Building) to hold all his Old Masters. In 1941, President Roosevelt formally accepted the building and all the treasures in it— 126 paintings, plus 26 sculptures—on behalf of the nation. Soon after, eight other industrialists and financiers, whom Mellon had previously tapped, added their collections to form the gallery's core. In 1999, the National Gallery opened its nearby Sculpture Garden, a peaceful landscaped setting, for its collection of modern sculptures that includes a pool that doubles as an ice-skating rink in winter. *Right:* In order to pay his rent at a pension in Brittany, Paul Gauguin painted *Self-Portrait* on a cupboard door in his landlady's dining room. The painting was eventually acquired by Chester Dale, a financier who owned railroads and utilities and married a painter who schooled him in the art of collecting. Almost every major artist at work in Paris from the mid-19th century to the mid-20th was represented in Dale's collection, all of which he generously turned over to the National Gallery.

This bronze statue entitled *Mercury,* probably the work of 17th-century Flemish sculptor Giovanni Bologna, was part of Andrew Mellon's original gift to the nation and graces the National Gallery of Art West Building's rotunda.

## The National Gallery of Art, East Building

By the 1970s, Mellon's idea of a national museum filled with treasures had more than taken hold—the National Gallery was in serious need of expansion. The problem was designing a building to fit the adjacent lot, an oddly trapezoidal patch. Modern master architect I. M. Pei met the challenge by erecting two interlocking triangles and setting them in alignment with what is now the West Building. The East Building's open interior spaces are the perfect setting for the outsized collection of moderns, including Alexander Calder's gigantic and specially commissioned red, black, and blue mobile, which floats above the atrium. There are five floors of modern masters here, including Picasso, Kandinsky, Miró, Motherwell, and Lichtenstein. The East Building, which opened in 1978, connects to the West Building by an underground passage featuring a glassed-in waterfall.

# THE WASHINGTON MONUMENT

Eighty-five years and two months after George Washington died, the monument to America's most esteemed president, lauded as a minor god in his time, was finally complete. As early as 1783, Congress had a memorial to Washington in mind, something vaguely equestrian, though there was also discussion of a mausoleum (vetoed by Washington's family, who refused to release the president's remains). At long last, in 1832, the centennial of Washington's birth, the Washington National Monument Society was formed. By 1836, it had collected $28,000, which was enough for commissioned architect Robert Mills to begin work.

However, the site turned out to be too boggy to support Mills's ostentatious design, which involved an obelisk rising from a Greek templelike colonnaded building and featured a statue of Washington in, of all things, a toga. Another more stable site was chosen, and on July 4, 1848, in an elaborate ceremony that drew 20,000, the cornerstone was finally laid. But no sooner had work begun than committee squabbles and a lack of funds halted construction. At the outbreak of the Civil War, Washington's monument was an abandoned 152-foot stub in the middle of a field in which cattle grazed and Army foot soldiers drilled.

When work resumed in 1876, engineers discovered flaws in the foundation and called for a retrofit, further slowing progress. By that time, all but the graceful obelisk that you see today had been, blessedly, eliminated. At last, on February 21, 1885, the day before Washington's 153rd birthday, the 555-foot monument, which is still the world's largest freestanding stone structure, was dedicated.

*Above:* Almost 30 years after work began, the Washington Monument was still under construction as seen in this photograph, circa 1876. At this point, the monument was only about 175 feet tall, which left another 380 feet to go. *Above right:* Contributors to the Washington National Monument Society, tasked with raising funds to erect the obelisk on the Mall in George Washington's honor, were awarded this membership certificate as thanks. The final cost of the monument came in at $1.8 million.

Every state of the Union has a memorial stone set inside the Washington Monument; the practice began when Alabama contributed the first stone in 1849. The stone shown here was offered by the Association of Journeymen and signifies the Stonecutters of Philadelphia. Soon, cities, counties, and even foreign countries sent memorial stones for installation along the monument's interior granite walls. There are 193 stones in all.

Construction on the Washington Monument stopped in 1854 due to fiscal problems and design modifications. By the time work resumed in 1876, it was discovered that the old marble didn't match the new. The result is a color shift noticeable at roughly the 150-foot mark.

Workers restore the capstone and apex of the Washington Monument in this photograph taken in the 1930s. Chunks of the Washington Monument's exterior had been steadily flaking off by the time restoration crews such as this one set to work. While the capstone (just beneath the platform on which the workers are standing) is made of marble, the pyramid-shape apex seen in the photograph is made of solid aluminum, considered a rare metal in the 1880s, when the Washington Monument was completed.

# THE LINCOLN MEMORIAL

When this grand neo-classical memorial to the 16th president was dedicated on Memorial Day 1922, it was nothing short of ironic that keynote speaker Dr. Robert Moton, president of the historically black Tuskegee Institute, was ushered into the segregated black section of the audience after he finished his remarks. Seventeen years later, on Easter Sunday 1939, 75,000 gathered at the Memorial to hear famed contralto Marian Anderson perform, their presence, in part, a protest against the Daughters of the American Revolution, who refused Anderson the use of their Constitution Hall for her concert because she was African American.

But by 1963, when 250,000 marched on Washington to hear Martin Luther King Jr. deliver his "I Have a Dream" speech, America's days of segregation were at last dwindling, with the Lincoln Memorial a fitting backdrop to that change.

Although in his heart Lincoln condemned slavery, his public response to the institution was more calculated and driven by the political expediency that allowed him to win the 1860 election, if not the complete confidence of the nation. No sooner had he been sworn in than seven southern states seceded to form the

Confederacy. The result was a Civil War that lasted four years and cost more than 600,000 lives, including Lincoln's own.

In 1867, Congress authorized a memorial to the fallen president but did nothing more toward its execution until the McMillan Commission of 1901—responsible for so much of the improvement seen on the Mall today—finally designated a site near the Potomac. After Congress approved architect Henry Bacon's design, construction for the memorial began in 1914. New England sculptor Daniel Chester French designed the statue within the memorial itself.

*Opposite:* Visitors gather at sunset on the steps of the Lincoln Memorial with its partial image shimmering in the Reflecting Pool. *Right:* Work began on architect Henry Bacon's design for the Lincoln Memorial in 1914. Inspired by the Parthenon, the memorial features 36 Doric columns, one for each state in the Union at the time of Lincoln's death. Inside, on the attic wall, are the names of each of the 48 states that were in the Union when the memorial was completed in 1922. Installed inside, in addition to French's fabled statue of the president, are the words from the Gettysburg Address and Lincoln's Second Inaugural Address, which are highlighted with murals painted by Jules Guerin.

Daniel Chester French was the best-known American sculptor of his day. He was commissioned in 1915 to create the statue of Abraham Lincoln that sits inside the Lincoln Memorial. This 19-foot-high figure of the beloved 16th president, his face set in contemplation, was carved from 28 blocks of Georgian marble. French, who had a deaf son and knew American Sign Language, included a personal touch in his masterwork, as an unconfirmed story goes, by positioning Lincoln's left hand to form the letter "A" and his right to form "L."

*Left:* Operatic singer Marian Anderson performs at the Lincoln Memorial in 1939. First Lady Eleanor Roosevelt arranged the performance after Anderson had been denied use of the DAR Constitution Hall because of her race. *Right:* Dr. Martin Luther King Jr. waves from the Lincoln Memorial steps to the crowd gathered on the Mall for the August 28, 1963, March on Washington. King's "I Have a Dream" speech, delivered to an audience of 250,000, propelled the civil rights movement and remains a landmark event in the city's history.

# THE JEFFERSON MEMORIAL

Thomas Jefferson was the nation's third president and was perhaps best known for negotiating the famous 1803 deal with Napoleon: the Louisiana Purchase, which increased the size of the nation by almost a million square miles. John Russell Pope, who was also known for his design of the West Building of the National Gallery of Art, designed the memorial to Jefferson and patterned it after the Greek Pantheon. It was a design that Jefferson, an architect who favored classical styles (as exemplified in his beloved Monticello home in Virginia), would surely have approved. Controversy, however, arose over the chosen site along the Tidal Basin: It required the removal of several prized cherry trees, which were a gift from Japan in 1912. When President Roosevelt ordered ground broken for the memorial in 1938, construction crews first had to confront several local matrons who had chained themselves to the tree trunks in protest.

In 1941, sculptor Rudolph Evans began work on the 19-foot statue of Jefferson set within the memorial. The memorial was dedicated in 1943.

*Above:* Work on the Jefferson Memorial, which actually began in 1939, was almost halfway complete when this photograph was taken circa 1940. *Left:* Two Marines guard the statue of Thomas Jefferson during the dedication of the memorial in April 1943 on the 200th anniversary of Jefferson's birth and just 17 months after America's entry into World War II. The statue seen here is actually a plaster cast painted to look like bronze, owing to the wartime restriction on the extraneous use of metals. After the war, the statue was cast in bronze and installed in 1947.

Thomas Jefferson's bronze statue presides in silhouette within the memorial erected in his honor. There are also four panels inside the memorial to the third President, engraved with his most prescient words, including these, excerpted from his 1785 *Notes on the State of Virginia:* "Commerce between master and slave is despotism." The remark is striking considering that Jefferson, author of the Declaration of Independence, owned some 200 slaves at the time of his death in 1826. Some historians posit that Jefferson ranked blacks lower on what he called his "scale of being" in order to square himself with slavery.

In 1934, Congress established the Jefferson Memorial Commission and hired John Russell Pope, the nation's preeminent classical architect, to design a monument in honor of the third president. Pope died in 1937, leaving the unfinished project to colleagues Otto Eggers and Daniel Higgins; President Franklin Roosevelt laid the cornerstone two years later. The memorial, finally completed in 1943, has a 129-foot-tall rotunda, and the whole memorial is fashioned of 31,000 tons of marble from Vermont, Georgia, and Tennessee, with limestone from Indiana. The memorial is situated along the Tidal Basin, nestled amid Washington's famous cherry trees.

# THE TIDAL BASIN AND THE CHERRY TREES

Part of a control project intended to prevent another flood like the one in the spring of 1881, when the Potomac swamped the Mall all the way to the foot of Capitol Hill, the Tidal Basin was dredged from the river's mudflats, allowing the tidal Potomac to drain into the Washington Channel. The Basin was a popular swimming spot until well into the 20th century, when the bathhouse was razed to make way for the Jefferson Memorial. By then, Washington's prized cherry trees had taken root along its banks.

The trees were a goodwill gift from Japan. Unfortunately, the first trees, shipped in 1910, were infested with insects. Three thousand replacements arrived two years later, and in a ceremony that has since evolved into the famous Cherry Blossom Festival, then–First Lady Helen Taft and Vicountess Chinda, the Japanese ambassador's wife, planted the first two Yoshino-variety cherries.

During World War II, vandals took axes to several of the trees. Then, in the 1990s, beavers gnawed through more of the horticultural treasures. Crowds have also stressed the trees, breaking off blossoms as souvenirs to the point where only about 100 of the originals remain. But growers at the National Arboretum have begun a program of cultivating replacement saplings, which were grafted from the original stock.

*Above:* Sightseers stroll along the Tidal Basin under the blooming cherries. Every year the National Park Service declares peak bloom when 70 percent of the Yoshino blossoms are open.
*Right:* Cherry blossoms of the Yoshino variety are dominant among the famed cherry trees of Washington. The trees grow to a height and spread of about 30 feet. Those surrounding the Tidal Basin have a life span of about 50 years, but with care, they can live to more than 100.

The 2004 Embassy of Japan Cherry Blossom Princess, Tomoko Shiojiri, lights a Japanese stone lantern from a Tokyo temple (one of two along the Tidal Basin). Since 1954, a woman related to a Japanese diplomat has been chosen to light the lantern to open the Cherry Blossom Festival. Every year, hundreds of thousands come to Washington to see the blooms and enjoy the festival, picking up guides and buttons (*right*) along the way.

Blooming cherry trees ring the Jefferson Memorial at the Tidal Basin.

*Below:* The Franklin Delano Roosevelt Memorial originally put little focus on Roosevelt as a polio victim, but modern-day advocates for disabled Americans felt it was necessary to highlight his handicap. They successfully pressed their case in Congress, which, in 2001, authorized adding a statue of FDR in his wheelchair. *Right:* The National World War II Memorial honors the 16.4 million Americans who served in the war and was dedicated in May 2004, nearly 60 years after the war's end. Fifty-six stone pillars represent every state and territory in the United States during the war and each is hung with a bronze wreath. The memorial also contains 24 bas-relief panels that depict America's strengths, along with the Freedom Wall that honors the memory of the men and women who died in service to their country.

# WAR AND REMEMBRANCE: FDR AND THE WORLD WAR II MEMORIALS

Years before he died, Franklin Roosevelt had strict instructions for his friend, Supreme Court Justice Felix Frankfurter: When the time came, any memorial erected in Roosevelt's honor should be limited to a desk-size granite block inscribed with his name and dates of birth and death (1882 and 1945) and installed in front of the National Archives. (In 1931, the Archives were part of the Works Progress Administration, one of Roosevelt's plans to bring the nation out of the Great Depression.) Fifty years later, a bigger, better memorial to the president, who also guided the nation through World War II, was dedicated, this one covering seven acres in West Potomac Park. It may have been grander than the president had in mind, but it seems to match his achievements and is reflective of his popularity. Roosevelt was the first president to run for and win a fourth term before the 22nd Amendment to the Constitution was enacted in 1951, limiting presidents to two consecutive terms.

As for the 16.4 million Americans who served under Roosevelt's command during World War II, the Mall's newest addition is a memorial to them. As has been the case with many of Washington's monuments, this one also involved design disputes, fund-raising challenges, and construction problems that dragged on, in this case, for 12 years. Austrian-born architect Friedrich St. Florian's open and airy plaza was finally dedicated on Memorial Day 2004. Designing around a once-neglected pool, St. Florian turned it into a place of rest and contemplation.

# BEARING WITNESS: THE UNITED STATES HOLOCAUST MEMORIAL MUSEUM

Since its opening in April 1993, nearly 30 million visitors have toured the Holocaust Museum, 90 percent of them, remarkably, non-Jews. While the systematic genocide of six million Jews during World War II may have been its impetus, the museum's success—through its exhibits, research facility, and education programs—rests in its mission of bringing conscience to bear on all acts of hatred, whether historic or contemporary.

The idea for the museum grew from President Jimmy Carter's expressed wish that all victims of the Holocaust be memorialized and that one of history's darkest times be turned into a force for promoting world peace. To that end, President Carter looked for guidance from Nobel Peace Prize winner Elie Wiesel, a Holocaust survivor himself, along with several others, including Nobel Prize laureate in literature Isaac Bashevis Singer and University of Notre Dame president Father Theodore M. Hesburgh. (Carter himself was awarded the Nobel Peace Prize in 2002, with the establishment of the Holocaust Memorial as one of his many efforts.)

In 1980, Congress deeded two acres of land for the museum. Funds, however—about $168 million in all—came exclusively from private donations. In 1989, construction finally began on a building designed by James Ingo Freed, who drew his inspiration from several Holocaust sites. A trip to the Holocaust Museum is a sobering experience, and nowhere is Washington quieter, the atmosphere more reverent.

Unfortunately, in June 2009, that reverence was broken when an 88-year-old man armed with a rifle burst through the lobby and opened fire, killing museum security guard Stephen Johns before being apprehended. A World War II–era neo-Nazi, his act was very pointedly in complete opposition to the museum's mission of peace.

*Left:* At the Holocaust Memorial Museum, sunlight illuminates a wall of photographs of members of various families from a single village, most of whom perished under the Nazi regime. *Above:* At another exhibit, visitors examine the photographs of the identification numbers tattooed on the arms of death camp prisoners. In its many unadorned collections, the museum makes personal the extent of the slaughter, often to chilling effect. *Right:* Every visitor is given an "Identifcation Card" that tells the story of a victim or survivor of the Holocaust.

# THE VIETNAM VETERANS MEMORIAL

The plan to memorialize those who died fighting the most divisive war in American history began after veteran Jan Scruggs saw Michael Cimino's 1978 movie *The Deer Hunter*. In this film, Vietnam vets, back home in Pennsylvania, attempt to reconcile their war experiences with life in their depressed mill town. This adjustment, as Scruggs understood, was among the major challenges facing many returning vets who had not, for the most part, received a hero's welcome, as returning World War II vets had.

By 1980, and with Congress's approval, Scruggs had secured a two-acre site on the Mall to erect a memorial. He also established the Vietnam Veterans Memorial Fund, which he still operates and which sees to memorial maintenance and educational programs. The winning design for the memorial was submitted by Maya Lin, an architectural student and the daughter of Chinese immigrants. Her austere, haunting design caused an uproar among critics, who preferred something more traditional. To assuage them, Frederick Hart's sculpture of three soldiers was installed nearby.

According to the National Park Service, though, it's The Wall (as the Vietnam Veterans Memorial has come to be known) that draws more visitors each year than any other Washington memorial. To date, about 50 million people have come to pay their respects, many of them leaving notes and personal mementos—so many, in fact, that Scruggs's foundation now maintains the collection in a warehouse in Maryland.

The Vietnam Veterans Memorial is a V-shape. Each arm of The Wall is 247 feet long and made of 74 black granite slabs inscribed with the names of more than 58,000 servicemen and women who died during the Vietnam War. The names are arranged chronologically, beginning in 1959—the year of the first American casualty—and ending in 1975, the year of the war's end. Experiencing The Wall, as its four million visitors each year can attest, is cathartic.

## The Korean War Memorial

The Vietnam Veterans Memorial was no sooner complete than it drew criticism from some who mistook The Wall's unique and simple design as an antiwar statement, though that had never been Maya Lin's intention. Lin, a 21-year-old Yale architecture student, had her design chosen from among 1,400 others submitted in a 1981 competition. She argued that embellishments to her memorial would only have detracted from the war's terrible effects and the memory of those who died. Nevertheless, the privately operated Memorial Fund commissioned Frederick Hart to sculpt the *Three Servicemen* (or *Three Soldiers*) to counterbalance Lin's design. Hart's statue, along with a flagpole, was installed near The Wall and dedicated in 1984. However, it omits any depiction of the women who played such a crucial role in the war. This, in turn, led to the installation of sculptor Glenna Goodacre's Vietnam Women's Memorial, dedicated in 1993.

The Korean War Veterans Memorial was dedicated in 1995 to honor the 1.5 million Americans who served (under the United Nations flag and alongside soldiers from 21 other nations) in the conflict that began in 1950. With the slogan "Freedom Is Not Free" inlaid in silver in its wall, the memorial is intended to evoke the spirit of patriotism that so defined the era. But the centerpiece is the Field of Service, where 19 statues of soldiers, airmen, and marines, crafted of stainless steel, seem to advance with caution toward an American flag. The sculptures are the work of Frank Gaylord, a veteran of World War II. The wall is the work of graphic designer Louis Nelson and features sandblasted images of nurses, doctors, and other support personnel—about 1,200 in all—who served in aid of the combat troops.

# ARLINGTON NATIONAL CEMETERY AND THE ARLINGTON MEMORIAL BRIDGE

Arlington National Cemetery lies in Virginia, just across the Potomac from the Lincoln Memorial, and its 624 acres are hallowed ground for some 300,000 presidents, justices, servicemen and women, and others who have served their country.

It was originally part of the plantation of Robert E. Lee, son of Revolutionary War hero "Light-horse Harry" Lee, who married Mary Anna Randolph Custis, great-granddaughter of Martha Washington. By the early 1860s, and with war coming, the plantation and its

mansion, Arlington House, had fallen into disrepair. In April 1861, Lee left to assume command of the Virginia forces, and by 1864, the federal government was forced to seize the property when Mrs. Lee refused to pay the taxes.

At the suggestion of Union Army Quartermaster-General Montgomery Meigs, who considered Lee a traitor, the land was consecrated as a cemetery, and the first war casualties were buried in Mrs. Lee's prized rose garden, within clear site of the mansion.

At the end of the war, with no home to go back to and no other prospects, Lee assumed the presidency of small Washington College, founded in 1749 in Lexington, Virginia. Today called Washington and Lee University, it was where Lee died in 1870 and was buried.

As a symbol of national reconciliation, Arlington Memorial Bridge, which links the Lincoln Memorial to Lee's Arlington House and the cemetery, was dedicated in 1932 and is considered the city's most beautiful bridge.

## Arlington: Home of Robert E. Lee

On June 28, 1864, Union soldiers, both white and black, are bivouacked at Arlington House, former home of Confederate General Robert E. Lee. Lee's 1,100-acre plantation was originally called Mount Washington, in honor of the great man to whom Lee was distantly related by marriage. Just two weeks before this photograph was taken, Arlington House was seized by the federal government and converted into a burial ground for the Union dead, reserving some of the acreage for what became known as Freedmen's Village. Here more than 1,000 former slaves established a settlement and were put to work farming government fields and tending to the cemetery grounds until 1890, when the settlement was disbanded. In the 1920s, restoration began on the house, which passed into the care of the National Park Service in 1934. In 1972, Congress officially christened it Arlington House: The Robert E. Lee Memorial.

Visitors gather at John F. Kennedy's gravesite in Arlington National Cemetery (*below*). Kennedy loved this beautiful view of the city from the Virginia side of the Potomac River and had once remarked that he wished he could have moved the White House to this spot, which is how the site came to be chosen for his grave.

A bugler salutes the fallen at Arlington National Cemetery (*above*). On average, two dozen burials are conducted every day, these under escort of the 3rd U.S. Infantry, known as "The Old Guard," whose members also serve as sentinels at the Tomb of the Unknowns (*right*). While most of the

gravesites are of the military personnel who have served in all the nation's wars—from the Revolutionary War to the present wars in Iraq and Afghanistan—many of the gravesites are of other notable Americans. This is where Pierre L'Enfant, friend of George Washington and the city's planner, is buried. It's also where polar explorer Admiral Richard Byrd rests, along with jazz legend Glenn Miller, mystery novelist Dashiell Hammett, and Merriman Smith, the journalist with the first story of John F. Kennedy's assassination. Smith was a UPI reporter in Dallas at the time of the assassination. He committed suicide in 1970.

## The United States Marine Corps War Memorial

The United States Marine Corps War Memorial, often referred to as the Iwo Jima Memorial, is on the far north end of Arlington National Cemetery in Virginia. It honors the memory of all U.S. Marines who have died in defense of the nation since 1775, the year the Corps was founded. The memorial depicts one of the Corps' most decisive victories: the battle fought on the Pacific island of Iwo Jima during World War II. The memorial, the work of sculptor Felix de Weldon, stands 78 feet high and includes statues of the five Marines and the lone Navy hospital corpsman as they raised the American flag atop the island's Mt. Suribachi, signaling that the Americans were slowly gaining the advantage over the Japanese. The battle, which began on February 19, 1945, lasted 36 days and cost almost 7,000 Marines their lives, including three of the six flag-raisers. Nearly all of the Japanese troops perished. War photographer Joe Rosenthal snapped the photograph on which de Weldon based his work—a photograph so compelling that Congress, with uncharacteristic swiftness, allocated funds for the memorial within days of the photograph's publication. *Below:* The Iwo Jima statue is shown as it was being installed on its pedestal in September 1954. The base is inscribed with the words "Uncommon Valor Was a Common Virtue."

Construction of the Memorial Bridge began in 1925 and was almost complete when this photograph was taken. The bridge, which includes a draw span that is no longer operable, was opened to traffic in 1932.

## The Memorial Bridge

The beautiful Memorial Bridge stretches 2,163 feet across the Potomac in a run of nine classically designed and granite-faced arches. It was completed in 1932 and connects the Lincoln Memorial with Arlington National Cemetery and Robert E. Lee's Arlington House in a symbolic gesture of post–Civil War reunification. Two gilded bronze equestrian statues by Leo Friedlander, entitled *The Arts of War,* flank the east end of the bridge, facing Arlington, while another pair of similar statues, these entitled *The Arts of Peace,* by James Earl Fraser, flank the adjacent entrance to Rock Creek Parkway, also on the Washington side of the Potomac. The four statues were dedicated in 1951.

# THE PENTAGON

What the Defense Department wants, it usually gets. What it wanted in 1941, as the nation geared for war, was to have all its workers in one location. At the time, employees of the War Department, as it was known then, were scattered all over Washington in 17 buildings, including private homes, apartments, and even rented garages.

The Department faced one problem: where to put what was sure to be a behemoth of a building. Army officers who were handed the challenge immediately looked across the Potomac to an asymmetrical five-sided site in Virginia, adjacent to Arlington National Cemetery and once part of Robert E. Lee's plantation. Then they gave George Edwin Bergstrom—part architect, part genius—a single weekend to come up with a design to fit it.

And Bergstrom did, though opponents squawked as soon as the plan was unveiled. First, they questioned the Department's need for such a building, and then they objected to the impact that something so large, squat, and lopsided would have on the cityscape. Eventually, another site was selected, one less obtrusive and more regularly shaped—although Bergstrom's original five-sided design remained essentially intact. Sixteen months later, at a cost of $83 million, the Pentagon was complete.

*Top:* An aerial view shows the Pentagon, which is located across the Potomac River in Virginia.
*Bottom:* The Pentagon, the world's largest office building, was rushed to completion in 1943, just 16 months after construction began. It sprawls over six and one-half million square feet and today provides office space for more than 24,000 military personnel and civilian contractors.

Nearly 60 years later, on September 11, 2001, five al-Qaeda hijackers commandeered American Airlines flight 77 and crashed it into the Pentagon, killing 184 and severely damaging the building. Repairs began at once and were completed exactly one year later, with a small, private chapel erected at the site of impact. Another memorial, the two-acre Pentagon Memorial Park, was opened to the public on September 11, 2008.

In October 1967, tens of thousands of peace demonstrators are gathered in front of the Pentagon building, in order to protest the war in Vietnam. The rally had begun on the Mall, and then the protestors walked all the way to the Pentagon, crossing the Memorial Bridge and causing traffic jams in the process.

Photographers view the collapsed side of the Pentagon four days after terrorists crashed a hijacked airliner into the building on September 11, 2001. Although the damage to the building was repaired quickly, the effect on the city has been lasting. Security is now a constant presence everywhere in Washington, especially at sites popular with tourists. As for the Pentagon, public tours have been permanently suspended.

# Washington's Evolving Downtown

Between the end of the Civil War and the beginning of the 20th century, Washington finally emerged as a city worthy of capital status. Members of Congress, dispatched to Capitol Hill to fulfill their legislative terms, and foreign diplomats, posted here from the world's most sophisticated cities, were less inclined to regard Washington as a backwater—its wide avenues were finally paved, tree-lined, and gas-lit, and its residential neighborhoods of townhouses and mansions were now fashionable.

Nowhere was Washington's vibrancy more evident than downtown, where F and G streets formed the shopping district's hub. Fine department stores, such as Garfinckel's, Hecht's, Palais Royal, Saks, Kann's, and Lansburgh's served as haberdashers to Washington's elite, also supplying them with furniture and housewares and serving them sandwiches in their tearooms.

None, however, was more successful than Woodward & Lothrop, which occupied an entire city block and a half, displacing an orphanage and a school in its expansion. Founded in 1880, Woodies, as it was known, was famous for its top service and its especially elaborate window displays at Christmas. With its flagship store as a Washington institution, Woodies

expanded, following its customer base into the suburbs. By mid-century, it had a branch in every major shopping center. But the 1970s brought a shift in retail from elegant upscale department stores to charmless big-box discount operations, and Woodies, its fortunes fading, gradually closed its stores and declared bankruptcy in the 1990s. Today, Macy's is the city's only downtown department store, supplemented by specialty shops and boutiques that have opened along the area's revitalized blocks, especially in downtown's Penn Quarter district.

## PENN QUARTER

Mostly a collection of government office buildings, Penn Quarter had a dreariness only offset by the grand Greek Revival-style Patent Office Building erected in

George W. Romney, former Governor of Michigan and one-time head of the Republican Party, addresses a gathering at the National Press Club as seen in this photograph from 1964.

*Opposite:* Woodward & Lothrop, shown here in the early 1900s, was once one of Washington's most fashionable department stores.

The National Building Museum's grand interior makes it a perfect spot for official gatherings of all kinds. Here, G20 leaders from around the world meet at the Summit on Financial Markets and the World Economy in November 2008.

1836. Until the Smithsonian opened its first museum in 1855, more than 100,000 people visited the Patent Office every year to see all manner of American invention on display—enough exhibits to circle the top floor of the Patent Office Building for a quarter mile. In the 1960s, the Smithsonian took over the building and opened both its American Art Museum and the National Portrait Gallery (keeper of all the official presidential portraits). By the 1990s, revitalization was in full swing in Penn Quarter, with 7th Street becoming its spiffy main thoroughfare. A mixed-use area of pricey condos, posh shops, and upscale eateries, the neighborhood also boasts the Verizon Center, a performance and sports venue,

and the International Spy Museum, which is devoted to all things espionage and occupies five of the once-dreary office buildings.

## ENTERTAINMENT AND TOURISM

By 1940, the city's population had grown to a little more than 600,000—roughly what it is today—with the federal work force about to rapidly expand with the onset of war. When they weren't working or shopping, Washingtonians took to the theaters. While the city lacked a reputation for cultural refinement—that would come later with the opening of the Kennedy Center in 1971—Washington had several theaters. Among them was the elegant Fox, later known as the Capitol, on F Street, with its marble staircase and its Wurlitzer, showcasing performers on the vaudeville circuit. The smaller but still elegant National and Warner theaters draw audiences today for one-man shows and Broadway-bound plays and revivals. But no Washington theater is better known than Ford's, which opened in 1863 and was the scene of Lincoln's assassination on Good Friday in 1865. Lincoln himself had been a theatergoer and had seen eight plays at Ford's. One of those plays, chillingly, featured John Wilkes Booth in the lead.

One of the unintended consequences of Lincoln's assassination was a rise in tourism that hasn't abated to this day. In a swell of post–Civil War patriotism, the curious flocked to Washington not only to visit the scene of Lincoln's tragedy but to tour the beautiful capital of one of the most powerful nations on earth. As tourism increased, the need for more hotels arose, especially classier establishments willing to cater to guests. Besides the Willard, near the White House, and the Hay-Adams, on Lafayette Square, there was—and still is—the grand Mayflower. It opened in 1925, just in time to host Calvin Coolidge's inaugural ball, and there's been a ball at the Mayflower for every inaugural since.

## POWER AND THE PRESS

The grandest inaugural ball is usually held in the National Building Museum between F and G streets, site of the former U.S. Pension Bureau, which administered military pensions. Since 1985, the building has operated as a center for public education on architecture and the building arts. It's an Italian Renaissance-style gem, the ceiling in its gilded Great Hall rising 159 feet and supported by eight Corinthian columns.

Of course, Washington isn't really about glamorous balls. It's a workaday town like any other, but its industry isn't heavy (which means that Washington is fairly clean and unpolluted, as cities go). Instead, it's focused on politics and the art of persuasion—or what has become known as lobbying. If the Founding Fathers believed in the right of the citizens to redress the government, they'd never believe what that right has led to today. K Street's hired guns—in the form of law firms, public relations agencies, trade associations, and membership groups—number well into the thousands, which is many times the actual number of senators and representatives whose votes they work to influence.

Trying to cover it all is the press, both national and international, with offices in the National Press Building. It opened in 1927, and its top-floor National Press Club is where the world famous, from Gandhi to Gorbachev, have addressed the press corp. As for the press in Washington itself, at one time the city had five dailies, including *The Washington Post*. That paper was launched in 1877 and secured its reputation nearly 100 years later with its exposure of the Watergate scandal that eventually forced the resignation of President Richard Nixon. *The Post* is now the city's only viable paper, still hanging on in this era of journalistic upheaval. If it folds, however, as did Washington's landmark department stores in the face of changing retail conditions, the effects would be far more damaging. The capital of the free world would be left without one of democracy's essentials: a credible press. Will former *Post* publisher Katharine Graham's maxim "that journalistic excellence and profitability go hand in hand" win out? Only time will tell.

Ford's Theatre underwent an extensive restoration in 2008 and today appears much as it did in the 1860s, with the presidential box on the right. Ford's offers a full schedule of performances that includes an annual presentation of *A Christmas Carol*.

# FARRAGUT SQUARE AND THE K STREET LOBBYISTS

Connecticut Avenue and K Street come together at Farragut Square, a park that forms the business district's hub and is popular with the lunchtime crowd. It was named for Admiral David Farragut, a Civil War naval hero famous for the capture of New Orleans and for the rallying cry attributed to him: "Damn the torpedoes! Full speed ahead!"

Most law firms and lobbying groups are clustered around the square where, some would argue, the real power resides in Washington. Influence peddling is, of course, as old as the nation, but it wasn't until after the Civil War, during the Grant Administration, that office-seekers and others with cases to press began flocking to Washington, victory in war having brought a sudden legitimacy to the capital. It was President Grant himself who called them "lobbyists," after their habit of gathering in the lobby of the Willard Hotel near the White House. In the years since, Congress has tried (and failed) several times to pass laws to limit lobbyists' influence, but conflicting interest among its members prevented the passage of any meaningful legislation until 1946. However, that law, which required registration and financial disclosure, was woefully inadequate.

And in 1991, a government report listing 13,500 Washington lobbyists showed that 10,000 of them were noncompliant. In 1995, Congress finally strengthened the law, though this did little to stop the Republican Party's Jack Abramoff. He pulled off possibly the lobbyists' grandest swindle when he defrauded four Native American tribes out of tens of millions of dollars during George W. Bush's presidency. Whether the lobbying laws were inadequate or not, Abramoff was imprisoned on felony convictions.

*Above:* Members of the Women's International League for Peace and Freedom rally in 1933 at the foot of the statue of Civil War hero Admiral David Farragut in the square named for him. *Left:* Today's Farragut Square is an oasis amid the plethora of new office buildings occupied by the law firms, trade associations, and lobbying operations that form the core of modern Washington's downtown.

# THE MAYFLOWER HOTEL

Claiming more gold leaf than the heavily gilded Library of Congress, the Mayflower was dubbed the "Grand Dame of Washington" when it opened in 1925, setting the standard for luxury. Every presidential inauguration features a ball at the Mayflower, and it was the hotel of choice for many, including Franklin Roosevelt, who retreated here to perfect his "We have nothing to fear" inaugural speech of 1933. Its posh Town & Country bar remains a favorite spot for trysts and K Street deal makers. It is also where FBI director J. Edgar Hoover ate lunch almost every day for 20 years. The Mayflower has catered to the illustrious, such as Queen Elizabeth and Barbra Streisand, and those somewhat less so: Bill Clinton paramour Monica Lewinsky stayed here when she was in town giving testimony to special prosecutor Kenneth Starr, and former New York governor Eliot Spitzer, registered as George Fox, met his call girl in room 871—an act that led to his resignation in 2008.

*Above:* The stately Mayflower Hotel, seen in this photograph circa 1916, is still a fixture on Connecticut Avenue. *Left:* President Kennedy addresses attendees at a prayer breakfast at the Mayflower Hotel in 1961.

## St. Matthew's Cathedral

The Cathedral of Saint Matthew the Apostle was founded in 1840 and has been at this Rhode Island Avenue site since 1893. Shown at left in 1960, its cruciform Romanesque red brick design is the work of C. Grant La Farge, known for his work on other churches, including the Cathedral of St. John the Divine in New York. Requiems have been held here for several notables, including President Kennedy. An inlaid marble plaque marks the spot where his coffin rested before the sanctuary gates and reads: "Here rested the remains of President Kennedy at the Requiem Mass, November 25, 1963, before their removal to Arlington where they lie in expectation of a heavenly resurrection." *Above:* Worshippers gather for Mass at St. Matthew's, which features a rare blend of yellow, green, purple, and white marble quarried in Switzerland, Italy, the United States, and North Africa. Murals and mosaics of angels and saints, notably Edwin Howland Blashfield's 35-foot-high St. Matthew, further adorn the walls, the chapels and altars, and the domed ceiling, which rises 190 feet.

# THE WASHINGTON POST

Founded in 1877 by journalist Stilson Hutchins, *The Washington Post* was, according to a contemporary account in *The Post* itself, "smart, funny, [and] plain-spoken," but also "frequently racist [and] sexist"—hardly possessed of the liberal bias it was criticized for in 2008. By 1890, *The Post,* under new ownership, was still a rag-tag operation when it turned to John Philip Sousa for help. A Washington native and head of the U.S. Marine Band—the hottest musical act in town—Sousa whipped up "The Washington Post March" as part of a promotional scheme to increase circulation. Both the song and the paper became wildly popular, but by the 1930s, the paper had fallen on hard times. Edward Beale McLean, a dapper playboy, was its publisher, though he took absolutely no interest in the news and would bring his mistress to staff meetings. Beale was caught with President Harding in the Teapot Dome scandal, where bribes were exchanged for private oil-drilling rights on the Teapot Dome Federal Reserve in Wyoming. Beale finally lost the paper, although his wife, the clear-headed Evalyn, had tried to save it by way of her own considerable wealth. Eugene Meyer, father of the legendary Katharine Graham, was *The Post*'s next owner, and under Meyer's leadership, the paper slowly regained its reputation. When the paper passed to Katharine Graham in 1963, it still wasn't the city's top news source. Its competition was most notably the popular *Washington Star.* Ironically, it was another scandal that finally secured *The Post*'s reputation: Watergate, first reported in 1972 by tenacious journalists Carl Bernstein and Bob Woodward. Graham's granddaughter, Katharine Weymouth, is publisher now, steering *The Post* through the challenges of the electronic age.

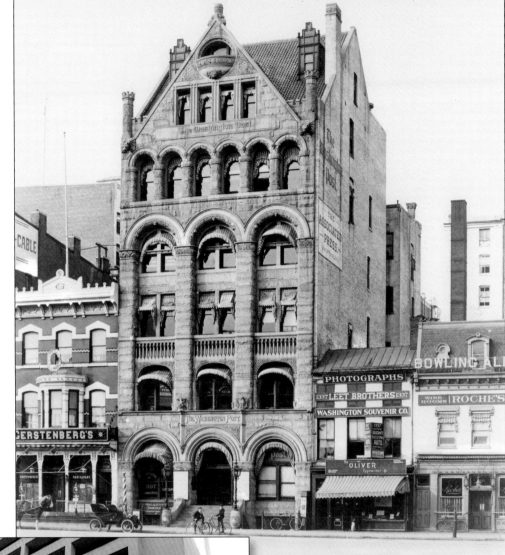

*Above: The Washington Post* has had several locations over its 133-year history, including this imposing Gothic-style headquarters on E Street NW, which the paper occupied from 1893 until its move in 1950 to L Street.
*Left:* Journalists and other *Post* employees gather in front of *The Washington Post*'s current headquarters at 1150 15th Street NW in 2009, in hopes of catching a glimpse of Barack Obama, who had just concluded a lengthy interview with the paper five days before his inaugural. Over its long existence, *The Post* and its team of outstanding reporters and photojournalists have won more than three dozen Pulitzer Prizes.

# THE NATIONAL GEOGRAPHIC SOCIETY

Founded in 1888 by a group of explorers and scientists at a private club on Lafayette Square, the National Geographic Society today is one of the world's largest nonprofit organizations for the advancement of science. It has funded more than 9,000 research projects and educational programs and—through its magazines, television channel, radio broadcasts, books, videos, and maps—has reached close to 400 million people worldwide. Gardiner Greene Hubbard was its first president, followed by Alexander Graham Bell, Hubbard's son-in-law. It was Bell's son-in-law, Gilbert Grosvenor, who served as *National Geographic* magazine's first editor, and whose family has played a prominent role in the Society ever since. Its ten-story downtown headquarters opened in 1964 and was designed by Edward Durell Stone, the avant-garde architect of the Kennedy Center. Explorers Hall, said to contain the world's largest free-standing globe, offers a regular schedule of free exhibits that have focused on everything from King Tut to space exploration.

*Left:* National Geographic's headquarters building, shown here today, houses the library, the news service, and the society's other administrative functions. The building became part of Washington lore when CIA agents were allegedly posted on the roof, observing the goings-on at the Russian embassy across the street. The Society's other more modern-style adjacent building is used as museum space to present an ongoing series of exhibits covering exploration, cultural artifacts, and photography. *Below:* The centerpiece of popular Explorers Hall is this free-standing globe, said to be the world's largest.

# THE NATIONAL PRESS BUILDING

This landmark building is home to news-gathering bureaus from across the globe, stationed in Washington to cover developments in the nation's capital. It's also the headquarters of the prestigious National Press Club, a professional organization for journalists that began in 1908 to "encourage friendly intercourse among newspapermen . . . and to foster the ethical standards of the profession." For years, members met in hotels and restaurants around town until, by the 1920s, membership expanded to the point where the club needed its own building. The 14-story National Press Building is on the site of the old Ebbitt House Hotel. Journalists as well as their sources are eligible to join the club, which hosts a series of luncheons and other events where newsmakers from around the world address the members. It is, as former CBS newsman Eric Sevareid once remarked, "the sanctum sanctorum of American journalists."

The National Press Building, seen here in 1963, has been at 14th and F streets since President Coolidge laid the cornerstone in 1926. The building was renovated in the 1980s, significantly modernizing the original limestone facade. Aside from press offices, the building has always had several popular ground-floor shops. Until 1963, it also housed the elegant Fox Theater.

# TWO FOR ONE: SMITHSONIAN'S AMERICAN ART AND PORTRAITURE MUSEUMS

The centerpiece of revitalized downtown's Penn Quarter district, the Donald W. Reynolds Center for American Art and Portraiture is part of the Smithsonian Institution and actually two museums in one building. This Greek Revival beauty was originally the Patent Office, dispenser of trademarks to all stripes of Yankee inventors whose gadgets were on display in the top floor Exhibit Hall, thus serving as a precursor to the Smithsonian Institution itself. Clara Barton worked here as a clerk to a patent commissioner before the Civil War, when the building was turned into a temporary barracks and a military hospital. Walt Whitman nursed and read to the wounded here, at the same time revising his *Leaves of Grass* for its 1867 publication. Lincoln's second inaugural ball was held here in March

1865, with 5,000 party crashers cheering the end of the Civil War and jamming the space prepared for 300 invited guests.

By the 1960s, the Smithsonian had acquired the building, with its curving double marble staircases and its stained-glass skylights. The building became the American Art Museum and the National Portrait Gallery, repository of the official presidential portraits as well as those of prominent Americans in every field. The building underwent an extensive renovation in 2006, heavily funded by the aluminum fortunes of the Reynolds family. It was reopened as the Donald W. Reynolds Center for American Art and Portraiture.

Political cartoonist Pat Oliphant, who has made a career of satirizing presidents, is also an accomplished sculptor. His caricature of George H. W. Bush shows the former president distracted from the demands of his office by a game of horseshoes. The bronze is positioned near Ron Sherr's portrait of George H. W. Bush and Henry C. Casselli Jr.'s portrait of Ronald Reagan. The works are part of the American Presidents Gallery, a permanent and popular exhibit at the National Portrait Gallery.

*Opposite:* The American Art Museum and the National Portrait Gallery are two of the Smithsonian's best off-the-Mall museums today. The American Art galleries include photographs, drawings, folk art, and ornamental furniture spanning three centuries. The National Portrait Gallery side of the building features images of Americans in the visual and performing arts—as well as in literature, politics, sports, and the sciences—who have contributed to our national culture. The top floor houses a glass-enclosed conservation center where visitors can watch preservationists at work restoring national treasures. *Above:* A statue honoring Louis-Jacques Mande Daguerre, inventor of the daguerreotype—an early photographic process by which images were printed onto iodized silver plates—today stands, fittingly, outside the National Portrait Gallery. This Daguerre monument is one among more than 700 monuments in the city, erected to honor notables American and foreign.

What had once been the South Hall of the U.S. Patent Office, shown in this early 20th-century photograph, is now a wing of the National Portrait Gallery.

## Where the Spies Are

During its opening celebration in 2002, spies, of a sort, scale the side of the International Spy Museum located in the revitalized Penn Quarter neighborhood (*below right*). The museum is not only one of the few privately operated attractions in Washington but also one of the few to charge admission. (All the Smithsonian Institution museums and the National Gallery of Art are free.) Even so, the Spy Museum draws a regular crowd of tourists and Washingtonians alike, here for the exhibits that cover everything from Cold War's U-2 pilot Gary Powers to World War I's notorious Mata Hari, to the Navajo Codetalkers of World War II, to modern-day turncoat Robert Hanssen, responsible for the worst breach of intelligence in American history. *Below:* The International Spy Museum's stated objective is to educate the public about the critical role that espionage plays in world events and to do it in a way that engages. Shown here in 2007, as part of its Operation Spy program, the museum invites visitors to assume the role of intelligence officers on a mission to stop black-market arms dealers in the fictional city of Khandar.

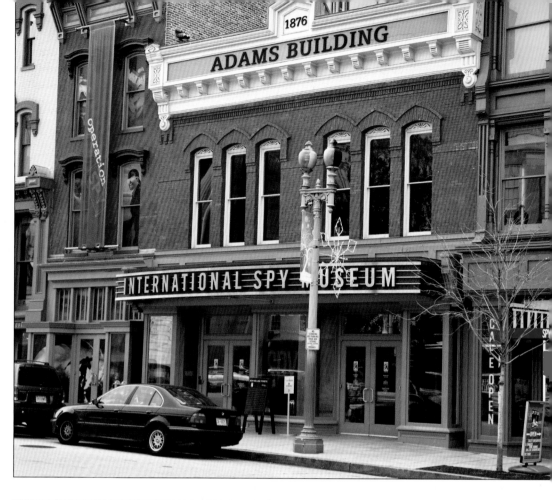

*Above:* The International Spy Museum occupies five former government office buildings in the Penn Quarter district. Its advisory board includes a mix of former FBI, CIA, and KGB agents who oversee the exhibits to ensure their authenticity.

## Carnegie Library

Pittsburgh industrialist Andrew Carnegie was the world's richest man when he retired from the steel-making business at the turn of the 20th century. He had amassed his wealth by less-than-scrupulous means, but Carnegie determined that he should give away most, if not all, of it. He funded many efforts with special emphasis on libraries, erecting 1,679 of them across the country. Above is the Carnegie Library that, from the day its doors opened in 1903 (shown here circa 1906), was desegregated. It served as the city's library until 1972, when the new Martin Luther King Jr. Memorial Library opened just a few blocks away. For years, the Carnegie Library sat basically abandoned until it underwent a $20 million renovation and reopened in 2003 as the new City Museum. It now holds the Historical Society of Washington's extensive collection of photographs and other artifacts pertaining to the city's history, and it features an ongoing series of exhibits and programs. *Right:* Martin Luther King III speaks in front of the library named for his father during the inaugural activities of President Obama in January 2009. The Martin Luther King Jr. Memorial Library is the city's main library.

# THE NATIONAL BUILDING MUSEUM

Derisively referred to as Meigs's Red Barn when it opened in 1887, the National Building Museum was designed by General Montgomery C. Meigs, an Army engineer who had also transformed Robert E. Lee's Virginia plantation into Arlington Cemetery. Inspired by the designs of Michelangelo, the building was a model of high-tech construction, complete with the latest in ventilation and fireproofing. It was built largely of red brick—15 million of them to be exact—which explains the nickname. The structure has a terra-cotta frieze that extends around the entire exterior and features sculptor Caspar Buberl's depiction of Civil War scenes.

By the 1960s, the building had fallen into disrepair and was ready for the wrecker's ball. Fortunately, it was saved by an act of Congress in 1978. Two years later, the National Building Museum was established, a nonprofit organization devoted to educating the public about architecture and the building arts. Since its restoration in 1997, the National Building Museum's Great Hall, with its gold leaf, center court fountain, and eight Corinthian columns, has been the site of the grandest of the presidential inaugural balls.

The National Building Museum occupies the block along F and G streets between 4th and 5th and serves as a center to promote the building arts. The red brick behemoth opened in 1887 and originally housed the U.S. Pension Bureau.

## WASHINGTON'S OLDEST SALOON

**WASHINGTON HAS MANY FINE EATERIES,** though few have lasted as long as the Old Ebbitt Grill, founded in 1856 by William Ebbitt, whose saloon and boardinghouse was originally located on the edge of Chinatown. Ebbitt's was known for its commodious lodgings, the quality of its food, and its good service, which attracted Washington's elite. Presidents Andrew Johnson, Ulysses S. Grant, Grover Cleveland, William McKinley, and Teddy Roosevelt all frequented Ebbitt's, where a printed blue card on each dining table read: "Many other famous statesmen, naval and military heroes, too numerous to mention here, have been guests of the house." Over the years, Ebbitt's moved several times, once to a location in the heart of downtown on F Street in what had once been a haberdashery. The Old Ebbitt Grill was especially popular with the lunchtime crowd, which would gather at the long wooden bar—decked out with beer steins and animal heads said to have been bagged by Teddy Roosevelt—to enjoy the choice hamburger platter. By the 1970s, as the focus began to shift away from Washington's old downtown to the newer office buildings along K Street and Connecticut Avenue, Ebbitt's became less popular and closure was imminent. That's when two enterprising restaurateurs bought the Old Ebbitt for a mere $11,000. In 1983, they moved it to its present location on 15th Street near the White House. Many of the original artifacts, including the wooden bar, didn't survive the move, although the beer steins did, as has the Old Ebbitt's spirit of hospitality and reputation for good food.

*Above:* The National Building's grand interior reflects the style of the Italian Renaissance and makes it one of Washington's premier party spaces, especially during the presidential inaugurals.

*Right:* President William Taft's 1909 Inaugural Ball was held at the Pension Building, now the National Building Museum.

# FORD'S THEATRE AND THE PETERSEN HOUSE

John T. Ford was a successful theatrical promoter from Baltimore when he came to Washington in the 1860s and converted a vacated Baptist church into a performance space. After fire destroyed the church, Ford rebuilt on the site, opening his quite-grand theater in August 1863. Until the assassination of President Lincoln forced him to close less than two years later, Ford staged 495 performances here, booking first-rate actors and routinely filling his seats with patrons glad for an evening's diversion during the terrible years of the Civil War. Although the federal government allowed Ford to reopen after concluding an investigation into the assassination, audiences weren't keen on the idea, some even threatening to burn down the theater. In 1866, Ford finally sold his theater to the government for $100,000; they used it for War Department office space and storage. And that might well have been the end of the tragedy at Ford's were it not for the 1893 collapse of three floors of the old theater caused by the weight of all those government documents. Twenty-two clerks were killed and another 108 were injured. In the 1930s, the National Park Service acquired the old theater and opened a small museum containing Lincoln artifacts. In 1968, after getting a good going-over, Ford's reopened, fully restored as a theater. The theater and the museum were upgraded in another major overhaul in 2008. As for Petersen House, where Lincoln died, doctors Charles Leale and Charles Taft, both in the audience at Ford's that night, carried Lincoln across the street to the home of William Petersen, a tailor, and laid the president across a bed in the back room where he died at 7:22 A.M. on April 15, 1865. Dr. Leale, only 23 years old and new to his profession, held the mortally wounded president's hand all through the night in hopes that Lincoln would at least know he wasn't alone.

*Above:* Sentries are stationed outside Ford's Theatre, which has been draped with black mourning crepe. President Abraham Lincoln was assassinated here by John Wilkes Booth on the evening of April 14, 1865. *Left: Our American Cousin,* a comedic farce, was on the bill at Ford's Theatre that fateful night in 1865, as shown on this program. The play featured popular British-born actress Laura Keene. She had no hand in Lincoln's assassination, but because her name was inexorably linked to the tragedy, her career all but ended.

*Right:* This photograph, taken circa 1865, shows the presidential box at Ford's Theatre, festooned with the American flag and marked with a likeness of first president George Washington, indicating that President Lincoln was in attendance.

*Left:* The mortally wounded President Lincoln was carried from Ford's Theatre, across 10th Street, to this home owned by William Petersen, a Swedish-born tailor. *Above:* Lincoln died in this back room of the house, his lanky 6-foot, 4-inch frame too long for the bed and thus laid diagonally across it.

## MARY SURRATT

**WHEN MARY JENKINS SURRATT RENTED A ROOM** in her H Street boardinghouse to John Wilkes Booth, she could never have predicted the tragic turn her life was about to take. Mrs. Surratt and her husband were prosperous farmers and innkeepers in nearby Prince George's County, Maryland. John Surratt's sudden death in 1862 left the widow with mounting debts and few resources other than the H Street house, which the couple also owned. The Surratts had been sympathetic to the Confederate cause, and Surratt's son, John Jr., was friendly with Booth and his associates when Mary moved to Washington and opened her boardinghouse. Two nights after the Lincoln assassination, as the search was on for Booth, Mary was arrested at her home and charged as a coconspirator. The evidence against her included the damning testimony of John Lloyd, the man Mary had asked to operate the Maryland property. Lloyd, a former police officer, produced evidence to show that Mary had instructed him to have supplies ready for Booth and his accomplices when they stopped at the farm during their escape through Maryland. The military court heard the case and quickly handed down the death penalty for Mrs. Surratt, as well as coconspirators Lewis Powell, George Atzerodt, and David Herold. All were hanged in the yard at Ft. McNair on July 7, 1865, making Mrs. Surratt the first woman to be executed by federal order. Her former H Street home, which bears a small plaque marking the building's historic significance, has long housed a popular Chinese restaurant.

The National Theatre has been a fixture on Pennsylvania Avenue since 1835, though it's now in its sixth incarnation—all five of the previous buildings on this site burned to the ground. The current theater, popular with touring companies of Broadway musicals, opened in 1923. A failed effort to integrate the theater led to its closure in 1948, but it reopened to audiences of all colors four years later, becoming one of the few desegregated public facilities in Washington at that time. As part of the revitalization of Pennsylvania Avenue, the National Theatre underwent a major renovation in the 1980s.

The Warner Theatre, originally the Earle, opened in 1924, offering vaudeville acts and silent movie screenings, with a rooftop garden, posh basement restaurant and nightclub, and its own troupe of chorus girls (the Roxyettes). By the mid-'40s, vaudeville acts were out, and the Earle switched exclusively to movies. Its name also changed to the Warner, after owner Harry Warner, one of the Hollywood Warners. Movies produced using "Cinerama," as advertised here in 1959, were showcased at the Warner, where blockbusters such as *Ben-Hur* enjoyed long runs. By the 1970s, the Warner became disreputable and, for a time, showed only pornographic films. The theater found new life in the late 1970s as a live concert venue but closed in 1989 for a three-year renovation. Its grand reopening was worth the wait—Frank Sinatra, in one of his last appearances, took the stage.

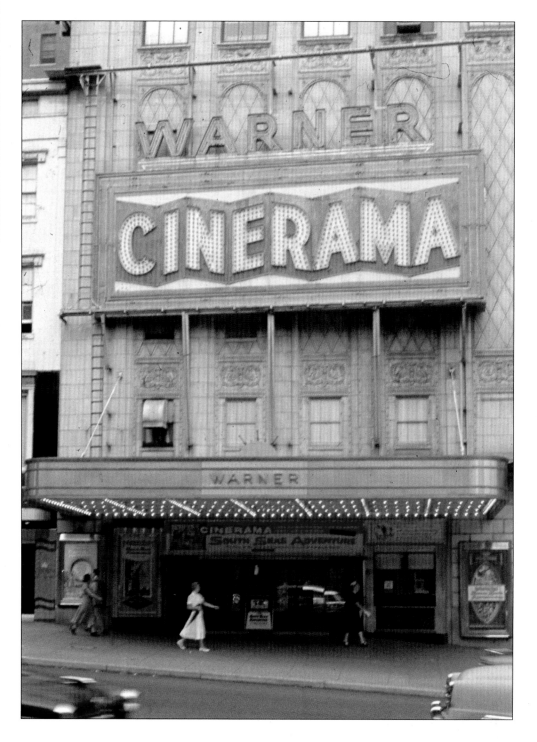

## Chinatown

Revelers celebrate Chinese New Year at the Friendship Arch that stands 60 feet above H Street at 7th, marking the entrance to Washington's Chinatown. The Arch was installed in 1986 to symbolize the link between capital cities Washington and Beijing. As Chinatowns go, Washington's has always been comparatively small, settled at the eastern edge of downtown during the early 20th century. It was made smaller still when, in the 1980s, developers targeted the area as the perfect place for the more economically viable Convention Center and the Verizon Center, a 20,000-seat sports arena. Home to the Washington Wizards, the city's basketball team, the Verizon Center also draws rock legends who perform here to sell-out crowds. But amid all the development, Washington favorites such as Tony Cheng's Seafood Restaurant and Mongolian Barbecue have remained intact.

The Washington Convention Center is officially named in honor of Walter E. Washington, the city's first mayor, who was elected in 1974 after Congress finally granted Home Rule to the city. The convention center is the latest in a series of halls built to accommodate huge indoor gatherings in Washington, the first of which was opened in the 1870s. Today's five-level convention center contains conference and banquet halls, classrooms, exhibit booths, and theaters, totaling nearly three-quarters of a million square feet of space.

## Foggy Bottom, Georgetown, and the Potomac

# Washington's Cultural Coming-of-Age

If you lived in Washington in the mid-20th century and wanted to take in a performance—whether a symphony orchestra, an opera, a ballet, or a quality theatrical production—you would have boarded a train at Union Station for Philadelphia, the nearest city with anything close to a vibrant cultural scene.

Washington may have had the Smithsonian Institution, with its wealth of historical and natural artifacts, and, by 1941, the National Gallery of Art, with its art treasures culled from the country's wealthiest collectors, but when it came to the performance arts, the city was shamefully lacking. Some foreign diplomats posted in Washington actually received "hardship duty" pay for having to serve in a city so culturally inferior. President Eisenhower felt the lack, too, and in 1958, he signed legislation that would eventually lead to the 1971 opening of the Kennedy Center, now one of the nation's top performance venues.

### FOGGY BOTTOM ELEGANCE

In its first ten years of operation, the Kennedy Center—inconveniently located amid a hard-to-navigate tangle of roads in the section called Foggy Bottom—drew 40 million people from all over the world to its six stages. Foggy Bottom got its unflattering name from the vapors that rolled off the Potomac, combined with those from the smoke-stacks of a brewery and a gas works that once dominated the neighborhood.

Foggy Bottom is also home to another important Washington landmark, though one of dubious distinction: the Watergate. A hotel, office, and condominium complex, the Watergate, all modern curves and tiers, came to public attention only a year after it opened, when the offices of the Democratic National Committee were burglarized in June 1972, marking the beginning of the end of Richard Nixon's presidency. Despite the unfortunate association, the Watergate has hung

Washington, D.C.'s Chain Bridge stretches over the Potomac, with the Chesapeake & Ohio (C & O) Canal in the foreground.

*Opposite:* The remains of 163 crew members of the USS *Maine*—which was blown up in Havana harbor sparking the Spanish-American War—were given a solemn funeral that included this procession along M Street on December 28, 1899.

Dumbarton Oaks owners the Blisses hired architect Beatrix Farrand to transform their 53 acres at the edge of Georgetown in 1920. She divided the acreage into "outdoor rooms" in complementary styles.

shrinking number of citizens largely became impoverished. The waterfront was a shabby jumble of warehouses and slaughterhouses, along with a cement works, a flour mill, a power plant, and an incinerator with smokestacks that were constantly belching.

Then in the 1930s and '40s came Franklin Roosevelt and the New Dealers—the well-educated who were from wealthy families and were looking to do good in Washington during the Depression and World War II years. Living space was at a premium in the city then, and so, with the preservationist spirit, the influx of new Washingtonians tackled the renovation and restoration of Georgetown. Some of the best and the brightest soon called Georgetown home, including John F. Kennedy, who lived with his wife at 3307 N Street before he became president. By the mid-1950s, Georgetown had been transformed into an official historic district.

## HISTORIC GEORGETOWN

In its early years, Georgetown was the site of one of the nation's most ambitious public projects, the C & O Canal, which would have linked the Chesapeake Bay to the Mississippi River had things gone according to plan. But the canal's promoters hadn't anticipated the success of the railroads, which doomed the canal project long before it was completed. The C & O is a tourist attraction today, its towpath popular with picnickers and joggers. It is included among the 50 or so houses, taverns, markets, shops, and other buildings of historic importance, including the Old Stone House on M Street, which dates from 1765 and is Georgetown's oldest home, and, perhaps most impressively, Dumbarton Oaks, built in 1801. It was acquired in 1920 by Mr. and Mrs. Robert Woods Bliss, a former ambassador and his wife, who turned the gracious mansion into a gallery for their collection of Byzantine and pre-Columbian art. They also transformed the once-barren grounds into gorgeous terraced gardens with fountains, pools, and even an orangery.

In the 1980s, Georgetown's powerful citizens association had much to do with blocking the expansion of Metrorail (the city's subway system) into their neighborhood, arguing that it would only invite the riff-raff or, at least, more of them. Thus, on any weekend or summer night, Georgetown's busy M Street and Wisconsin Avenue are jammed with cars, the sidewalks packed with bar-hopping students and tourists in flip-flops. Not all change is bad, though, because due to the transformation of Georgetown's waterfront—along and below M Street—in the 1980s and '90s, it has become a thriving commercial center that includes a shopping mall, hotels, boutiques, and

on to its high-end status as one of the city's best addresses, though the future of the hotel, which went into receivership in 2009, is uncertain.

## GEORGETOWN

By the 1970s, as the city was establishing its cultural bona fides, Georgetown— once a thriving tobacco port—had reinvented itself as the city's most fashionable neighborhood. Originally part of Maryland, the town was established in 1751. By the 1790s, it had been incorporated into the new federal district and then fully absorbed by the city itself after the Civil War.

In the decades following the Civil War, Georgetown's shipping trade substantially declined, and its blocks of elegant Georgian mansions and Federal-style townhouses fell into neglect as its eateries, all of which may add to the congestion but are a vast improvement over the old watefront.

## POTOMAC, PALISADES, AND GLEN ECHO PARK

Upriver from Georgetown, the Palisades is a charming, mostly residential neighborhood overlooking the Potomac River, which was once popular as a summer retreat. It's not far from Great Falls, where in spring, the river gushes over the jagged rocks. The Potomac is Washington's most important natural feature—though runoff and industrial discharge made it unsafe for years. Today, it has been largely cleaned up and is popular with recreational boaters.

It's only a short ride from the Palisades to Glen Echo, an amusement park with a long history. Its Spanish Ballroom still draws weekend crowds, and, of course, it has the requisite, fully restored carousel. At the height of its popularity in the 1930s and '40s, thousands crowded into Glen Echo every weekend for the rides and the big-band concerts. Even though those concerts weren't as highbrow as those of the Kennedy Center's a few decades later, there was no doubt that they were fun. And if there was anything Washingtonians needed in those desperate days of the Great Depression and World War II, it was a little more fun.

A barge waits to pass through a lock on the C & O Canal. In the 19th century, barges passed through a system of 74 lift locks, raising the vessels from near sea level at Georgetown to an elevation of 605 feet at the terminus in Cumberland, Maryland.

# STATE DEPARTMENT WELCOME

After World War II, the State Department moved out of its dowdy Old Executive Office Building headquarters next to the White House and into sleek new Foggy Bottom digs. All steel and glass, the building is boxy and undistinguished. It gives no hint, from the outside at least, of American craftsmanship, presence, style, or history. The interior, however, tells a different story.

When they opened in 1961, the eighth-floor Diplomatic Reception Rooms—the official setting for receiving heads of state, foreign ministers, and royalty—had all the charm of an airport terminal with their concrete floors and exposed metal beams. Then deputy chief of protocol Clement Conger, with architect Edward Vason Jones, transformed them. With no formal training in antiques or preservation, Conger set to work paneling the walls, carpeting the floors, and filling the Reception Rooms with, to name a few, Chippendale chairs, Townsend-Goddard tables, mahogany sideboards, as well as a Bombe chest. The finely crafted 18th- and 19th-century American treasures total more than 4,500 pieces in all and are valued today at more than $100 million. And Conger did all this without spending a single public dime. Instead, he convinced his moneyed friends and acquaintances to give up their goods for the good of the nation, a tactic that earned him the nickname "The Grand Acquisitor." The transformation and maintenance of the Reception Rooms (which include a gallery, drawing rooms, and a dining room) are ongoing; they are still the setting for official State Department functions. They are also open to the public, though few are aware of it, which makes a tour one of Washington's best-kept secrets.

Located next to the White House, this Second Empire-style office building (left, in a drawing from 1898) was once shared by the War, Navy, and State departments. But in the years following World War II—while the United States emerged as the world's dominant power, and its diplomatic mission expanded—the State Department outgrew the building, which by then had become dated and derelict. Known today as the Old Executive Office Building, it has been completely restored to its original glory. In the meantime, the State Department moved to the considerably less elegant but far more functional box of a building on C Street, where it remains today (*above*).

The Diplomatic Reception Rooms, on the top floor of the State Department, are where the Secretary of State and other Cabinet members entertain official guests of the nation. The rooms are outfitted with crown moldings, inlaid floors, and dazzling chandeliers.

# THE WATERGATE

"Five Held in Plot to Bug Democrats' Office Here" was the headline on the front page of *The Washington Post* on Sunday, June 18, 1972. It was the first in a series of stories that would lead intrepid young reporters Bob Woodward and Carl Bernstein to investigate the cover-up in the Nixon administration that would result in the president's resignation on August 9, 1974.

The "Here" in the headline was the Watergate, a hotel, office, and condo complex. Designed by Italian modernist Luigi Moretti, Watergate went into construction in 1964 and was completed only a year before Nixon associates of the Committee to Re-elect the President,

or aptly, CREEP, broke into the offices of the Democratic National Committee (the committee had rented space at the hotel in order to organize for the 1972 presidential election).

Although President Nixon's resignation finally ended the scandal that distracted the nation for two years, the term "Watergate" is now a fixture in the American political lexicon, freighted with the skepticism that has since characterized our public discourse. But the Watergate itself has remained a tony address for many of the city's influential people, such as former Senators Robert and Elizabeth Dole and Supreme Court Justice Ruth Bader Ginsberg.

*Top:* The Watergate is located in Foggy Bottom near the banks of the Potomac. As the city underwent modernization in the 1960s, the Watergate was built as a high-density, self-contained urban village with its own shops and restaurants. Shown here today, it's a stop on the tourist bus route. The name comes from the "water gate," an arc of stone risers flanking the west side of the Memorial Bridge. Until the 1960s, a barge with a band shell would anchor in the Potomac, and bands would give free concerts for audiences gathered at the water gate. *Bottom:* Reporters Bob Woodward, at left, and Carl Bernstein are at work in *The Washington Post*'s newsroom in this 1973 photograph.

# THE JOHN F. KENNEDY CENTER FOR THE PERFORMING ARTS

The Kennedy Center is the fulcrum of the city's cultural life. Each year it offers more than 3,000 performances, drawing audiences of more than two million into its six theaters. It offers dozens of arts education programs, lectures, and free, and low-cost events, and is home to the world-class National Symphony Orchestra.

Like all things in Washington, however, it took an act of Congress and then-President Dwight Eisenhower's signature on the 1958 legislation before the building of the Center could even start. The National Capital Center for the Performing Arts, as it was originally called, was intended to be on the Mall—on the site that the Smithsonian's Air and Space Museum now occupies—but was moved to a crescent-shape ten-acre lot along the Potomac in Foggy Bottom after pro-Smithsonian forces won out. Ground

was finally broken in December 1964, but obstacles soon arose. Architect Edward Durrell Stone's design proved challenging to construction engineers, and then there were funding problems. Congress was hesitant to underwrite anything cultural, leaving most of the funding to private donors, whose contributions totaled $75 million. The center finally opened in September 1971, by which time legislation had been passed to rename the Center for President John F. Kennedy.

President Kennedy was a fervent booster of the center and hosted White House luncheons and receptions to enlist the help of business leaders. As he expressed it in November 1962: "I am certain that after the dust of centuries has passed over our cities, we, too, will be remembered not for victories or defeats in battle or in politics, but for our contribution to the human spirit."

*Top:* The Master Chorale of Washington rehearses at the Kennedy Center's Concert Hall in 2008. Elegant and acoustically perfect, the concert hall is the largest of the six performance spaces, with seating for more than 2,400. The concert hall is also outfitted with a 4,144-pipe organ, situated behind the stage, which was a gift from the Filene Foundation; its Hadelands crystal chandeliers were a gift from Norway. *Bottom:* The Kennedy Center occupies a site along the Potomac River once home to one of German immigrant Christian Heurich's brewery.

# THE PALISADES

When Captain John Smith sailed up Chesapeake Bay and then into the Potomac in 1608, there were already several Algonquin villages established along the Palisades. Land grants and encroaching settlers gradually displaced the natives, but almost 200 years passed before anyone built a permanent home there. That anyone was Abner Cloud, a miller from Pennsylvania who opened his flour mill and built a simple two-and-a-half story stone house in 1801, along what would eventually become the C & O Canal.

Several dairy farms, slaughterhouses, and Abner Cloud's mill were the mainstays in the Palisades until Henry Foxall, a newly arrived English industrialist, opened a foundry to produce cannons for the federal government in 1812, the same year Cloud died, marking the area's shift away from the pastoral and toward the urban. But that shift has been gradual. For years, the Palisades, with its cool breezes off the Potomac, was a refuge for Washingtonians escaping the city's unrelenting summer heat. Development didn't begin in earnest until the 1880s and was ongoing well into the 1960s. Although, like all Washington neighborhoods, its main arteries are now clogged with commuter traffic, and although it bears the additional burden of sitting directly beneath the noisy flight path of nearby National Airport, the Palisades has hung on to its charm. Its streets are still leafy and lined with a mix of shops and houses, from the early row houses on Elliott Street to developer Jacob Clark's imposing Romanesque mansion on Reservoir Road, which is now home to the Lab School, much lauded for its work educating children with learning disabilities.

The Abner Cloud House, built in 1801 and shown here in 1963, is the oldest in the Palisades and predates the adjacent C & O Canal by almost 30 years. Cloud lived here with his wife, Suzanne, and together they operated a flour mill until his death in 1812. Although the house and the mill passed out of the Cloud family, the mill was still a concern into the 1880s. Today, the National Park Service, which acquired and restored the property in the 20th century, operates it as part of the C & O Canal National Historic Park.

## Across Chain Bridge

Chain Bridge, just above Georgetown, spans the Potomac between the Palisades and McLean in Virginia. In this Civil War–era photograph, Union soldiers patrol the bridge, a strategic link between Washington and the Confederacy. The present-day Chain Bridge is thought to be the eighth built here on the narrows. The first was built in the late 18th century—it, and all the others, succumbed to floods. The current structure, designed using more advanced engineering, was built in 1939. Today, Chain Bridge is on one of the major commuter routes into Washington from the Virginia suburbs.

# THE POTOMAC RIVER

The Potomac River flows 383 miles from headwaters in West Virginia's Alleghenies, down through the piedmont and out into the Chesapeake Bay. Its name derives from an Algonquian word related to trading that 18th century Americans, including George Washington, spelled "Patowmack." By the late 1800s, "Potomac" was in common use; the U.S. Board on Geographic Names finalized this spelling in 1931.

Washington realized the river's commercial importance. In 1784, he organized the Patowmack Company, which carried goods and people by longboats through a series of canals between Georgetown and Cumberland, Maryland, to the northwest.

Except for the portion of the river that falls within Washington, D.C.'s boundaries, legal control of the Potomac over the last 400 years has shifted between neighboring Maryland and Virginia in an ongoing series of disputes. But no matter who had control, industrial discharge, sewage, and agricultural runoff polluted the Potomac for everyone. As late as the 1980s, even a wade in the river, with its dead fish and its algae blooms, almost guaranteed contraction of a life-threatening bacterial infection.

Today, thanks to a herculean cleanup effort and strict ongoing management, the Potomac is not only a clean water source for Washington but also a favorite with area boaters and university crew teams.

Theodore Roosevelt Island is an 88-acre wooded sanctuary in the middle of the Potomac between Foggy Bottom and Arlington, Virginia. The island was set aside in 1932 to honor the 26th president, who was a sportsman and naturalist. During his tenure, Roosevelt established the U.S. Forest Service; created more than 150 national parks, forests, and wildlife preserves; and issued executive orders to declare natural sites as national treasures. Along with several wooded trails, the island features a memorial plaza with fountains and a sculpture of Roosevelt by Paul Manship.

Fletcher's Boat House, shown here circa the 1960s or '70s, offers canoes, kayaks, and other sporting equipment for day-trippers exploring the Potomac and the C & O Canal. Fletcher's has been on the edge of Canal Road since 1850. Thompson Boat Center, which opened in 1952, is the area's other best-known rowing facility and is located downriver at the mouth of Rock Creek.

## Great Falls

A sportsman takes in the gushing Potomac at Great Falls, upriver from Washington. The falls and the surrounding Great Falls Park (on the Virginia side) and the C & O Canal National Historic Park (on the Washington and Maryland side) are popular with boaters, rock climbers and history buffs. In the late 18th century, the Patowmack Company managed a series of five canals around the falls, shipping goods between Georgetown and the Allegheny Mountain outpost of Cumberland, Maryland, in an effort to stimulate commerce between the settled east and what was then considered the frontier. As part of the effort to increase trade, a small town called Matildaville was established near Great Falls on the Virginia side and flourished until the 1820s. Great Falls is beautiful but dangerous due to poisonous copperheads, poison ivy, ticks, and other hazards, including the falls themselves. Every year, rescue teams fish out hikers, anglers, inexperienced boaters, and others who have slipped into the backwash.

Two crew teams row across the Potomac from the Virginia shore with the Watergate, the Washington Monument, and the Kennedy Center in the background on the Washington side. Various local jurisdictions that claim ownership of stretches of the shoreline haven't been able to coordinate efforts to commercially exploit the Potomac waterfront. Thus, except for Georgetown, the riverfront has remained largely undeveloped. That has proven to be a good thing—the Potomac and the surrounding wetlands are not only popular with crew teams and other recreational boaters but have become a haven for several varieties of wildlife, including bald eagles.

# GLEN ECHO PARK

Although it's in Maryland, Glen Echo Park has long been a Washington favorite. Glen Echo opened in 1891 on 516 acres owned by two brothers, the Baltzleys, who made it big on sales from their new-fangled kitchen gadget, the eggbeater. Thousands filled Glen Echo's amphitheater, then one of the world's largest, to hear lectures and enjoy performances. But after two seasons, the Baltzleys, who had overextended themselves with ambitious plans for further development, lost the park.

After a transfer of management, Glen Echo became a successful "trolley-park," in the mold of Chicago's Riverview and Pittsburgh's Kennywood, and by the 1920s, it was drawing crowds of four million every year. Patrons came for the bumper cars, the human roulette wheel, and the carousel, which operates to this day.

The park's Spanish Ballroom opened in 1933 and still attracts a regular crowd of weekend dancers. But Glen Echo was segregated. In the early 1960s, a group of Howard University students pressed for access and won, but when a riot broke out in 1968, Glen Echo was closed. It languished for years until the National Park Service took it over. Today, Glen Echo is operated in partnership with local government and citizens' groups as both an amusement park and an arts center where every year, half a million visitors enjoy classes, workshops, performances, and, of course, the carousel.

Welcome to Glen Echo Park! Until the 1960s, you could ride the streetcar to this end-of-the-line amusement park in nearby Bethesda, Maryland, which is still popular with families. It's only a few miles outside the city, but Glen Echo has always been worlds away in fun.

## Glen Echo Park Historic Season Opening

Two ten-year-old boys enjoy a ride on the carousel at Glen Echo in the spring of 1961, which marked the official opening of the amusement park's first nonsegregated season. But the fun didn't last. Racial tensions plagued the park until the 1968 riots, which left much of the city devastated and also closed the park.

*Below:* In 1956, the 12-year-old son of Indonesian then-President Achmed Sukarno makes the most of his ride in a bumper car at Glen Echo, while a girl in the background gets a little help with her car.

## Painted Ponies

The painted ponies of Glen Echo's Dentzel carousel have been going up and down and around and around for almost 90 seasons, each horse a classic example of the hand carving made famous by the Dentzel family whose carousel business began in Germany in the 19th century. Dentzel immigrants brought their traditions with them to Pennsylvania where they established their business—which is still going strong—and expanding it to include other examples of fine woodworking. Glen Echo's Dentzel carousel, which has been recently restored, was installed in 1921.

# GEORGETOWN AND KEY BRIDGE

No one really knows if Georgetown was named for its original landowners, George Gordon and George Beall, or for George II, on the throne in 1751 when the town was established. In either case, situated on the fall line as far up the Potomac as ships could then sail, Georgetown provided good harbor and, thanks to the popularity of tobacco, became one of America's busiest ports. Wealthy merchants and ship owners built their homes on the rise above the waterfront. There were several newspapers, shops, banks, and, of course, taverns, which, in those days, also served as makeshift community centers. Suter's

was one such tavern, where George Washington met with several Georgetown landowners in the 1790s, striking the deal that would add their acreage to the new federal territory.

Georgetown thrived until the rise of the railroads and the gradual silting of the Potomac, which reduced the river's navigability and forced the area into decline after the Civil War. The area remained in decline until Roosevelt's New Dealers, who arrived in the 1930s and '40s and were desperate for affordable housing, transformed blighted Georgetown into a historic district.

Today, Georgetown remains the city's most fashionable neighborhood. It links to Virginia by way of Key Bridge, named for Francis Scott Key, a lawyer who lived on M Street in the early 1800s and the author of "The Star-Spangled Banner." Key's lyrics, written during the War of 1812 to the tune of a British drinking ditty, did not become the nation's anthem until 1931, when, during the Depression, the country seemed in serious need of a unifying song. As for Key Bridge, it was completed in 1923 and is Washington's oldest surviving Potomac crossing.

Key Bridge, designed by Nathan C. Wyeth in the Classical Revival style, links Georgetown with the high rises of the Rosslyn neighborhood of Arlington, Virginia (background). Francis Scott Key (1779–1843) was a lawyer and sometime poet whose greatest inspiration came as he watched the British bombard Fort McHenry in Baltimore during the War of 1812. He lived in a brick home adjacent to the bridge that now bears his name. For a time in the early 20th century, Key's home was an American flag factory, but it fell into neglect and was finally torn down in 1949 to make way for the Whitehurst Freeway. A small memorial park now marks the site.

Wisconsin Avenue—seen today during the Christmas season—intersects M Street, with the two forming the commercial core of Georgetown. As the neighborhood's popularity grew during the mid- to late-20th century, so did Georgetown's traffic, which is constantly heavy.

The side streets off Georgetown's busy M Street and Wisconsin Avenue are lined with 18th-century Federal-style buildings, many still used as private residences, though some have been converted into charming shops and restaurants.

## THE EXORCIST STEPS

WASHINGTON, D.C., HAS BEEN THE SETTING for some of Hollywood's best-known films: dramas *(A Few Good Men)*; classics *(Mr. Smith Goes to Washington)*; thrillers *(No Way Out)*; and comedies *(Night at the Museum: Battle of the Smithsonian)*. However, it may be *The Exorcist* that Washingtonians regard as the most memorable, due to those wicked stone steps—97 of them—down which beleaguered Father Karras, his faith in crisis as he struggles to exorcise the demon in young Regan MacNeil, plunges to his death. Since the film's release in 1973, the steps (which rise near Key Bridge and connect M Street to the bluffs above the Potomac) have become a minor tourist attraction and part of Georgetown lore. Many of the movie's scenes were filmed on the campus of Georgetown University and at a brick house at 36th and Prospect streets, near the top of the steps. The brick house, where the exorcism occurs, was built in the 1950s on the former site of a Gothic-style Victorian once home to Mrs. E.D.E.N. Southworth, a long-forgotten novelist popular in the 19th century. In the movie, the priest crashes through the window of the house and onto the steps, giving viewers the impression that the two are adjacent, though, in fact, they are not. Clever work on the part of set designers and film editors links these two otherwise unassuming locations, heightening the film's chilling effects. All cinematic significance aside, "*The Exorcist* steps," as they are known, are actually hard to spot, because they are wedged between a brick commercial building and a stone wall and sit next to—most mundane of all—a gas station.

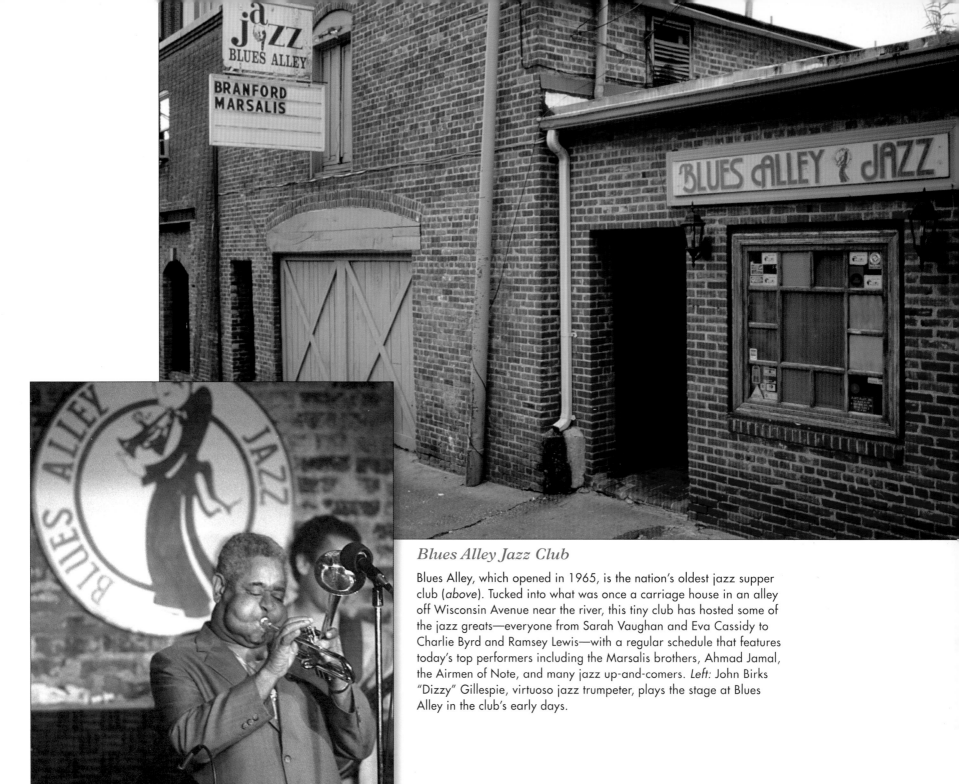

### Blues Alley Jazz Club

Blues Alley, which opened in 1965, is the nation's oldest jazz supper club (*above*). Tucked into what was once a carriage house in an alley off Wisconsin Avenue near the river, this tiny club has hosted some of the jazz greats—everyone from Sarah Vaughan and Eva Cassidy to Charlie Byrd and Ramsey Lewis—with a regular schedule that features today's top performers including the Marsalis brothers, Ahmad Jamal, the Airmen of Note, and many jazz up-and-comers. *Left:* John Birks "Dizzy" Gillespie, virtuoso jazz trumpeter, plays the stage at Blues Alley in the club's early days.

## On the Waterfront

Leisure boats anchor along Washington Harbour, an upscale complex of condos, shops, restaurants, and offices in Georgetown. Originally a thriving 18th-century tobacco port, Georgetown's waterfront remained industrial well into the 20th century. There were slaughterhouses here along with coal storage terminals, a flour mill, an incinerator, and, until the 1960s, a terminal building for the area's streetcar lines complete with a continuously belching twin-stacked powerhouse. The terminal building, a Romanesque behemoth built in 1895, was then converted into a car barn for the city's buses and has since been made over into an upscale office building. As for tony Washington Harbour, it's certainly an improvement over the lumberyard and the barge and dredging operation previously on the site.

The atrium at Georgetown Park Shopping Mall, at Wisconsin Avenue and M Street, is all fountains and flowers, wrought iron and skylights. This Victorian-style mall in the heart of Georgetown features 85 shops and restaurants and is on the site of what was originally stables and a waterfront warehouse. Later the area became a classified storage annex for the Pentagon.

School children on a field trip look on as boatmen instruct them in life on the canal. By the time this photograph was taken at the turn of the 20th century, the C & O Canal had long passed its prime, done in by the success of the railroads and the growing popularity of the automobile.

# THE C & O CANAL

The "Great National Project," as the C & O Canal was known, was intended to link the Potomac River and the Chesapeake Bay in the east with the Ohio River and Pittsburgh in the west, thus providing access through the Allegheny Mountains and on to the Mississippi. At the time, it was an ambitious undertaking—a 460-mile-long canal expected to take ten years to build and cost about $3 million—and it was plagued from the start. Labor troubles, engineering challenges, a shortage of funds, and disease all worked against the

project. Worst of all, competition from the new Baltimore and Ohio Railroad (for which construction began on July 4, 1828, the very same day ground was broken on the canal) made the C & O obsolete before it even opened.

In 1850, 22 years later, crews were still slogging away on the C & O, which was terminated at Cumberland, Maryland, a good 275 miles shy of the Pittsburgh mark, and with cost overruns that put a $13 million price tag on the unfinished

project. The C & O opened anyway and somehow stayed operational, if not always profitable, for the next 75 years, with a series of storms and floods finally forcing its closure in 1924. It sat neglected until the 1950s, when Supreme Court Justice William O. Douglas, an early environmentalist, rescued it from a campaign to pave it and turn it into a highway. The C & O, one of the last vestiges of early-American know-how and derring-do, was declared a National Historic Park in 1971.

Costumed interpreters guide tourists along the C & O Canal in *The Georgetown,* one of two replica canal boats operated by the National Park Service. The C & O is one of Washington's tourist attractions, with mule-powered boat rides offered in season from the Georgetown terminus and at Great Falls.

## Washington's Canals

A throwback to the 19th century, the C & O Canal and its towpath offer welcome respite in otherwise buzzing Georgetown. Another canal, a little more than a mile long, linked the C & O in Georgetown to the Washington City Canal, which in turn flowed through downtown Washington and across the Mall near the Capitol before emptying into the Anacostia River near Fort McNair. Although intended to spur commerce between the west and east ends of the city, the Washington City Canal was more a combination open sewer and mosquito hatchery. It was finally filled in during the 1870s, although underground portions still serve as part of the city's sanitary system.

# MT. ZION CHURCH AND GEORGETOWN'S BLACK HISTORY

Between its mid-18th century founding and its mid-20th century gentrification, Georgetown had a significant African American population. Slaves and freed men built the grandest of the capital city's public buildings, such as the White House and the Capitol, and labored on Georgetown's wharves. They also worshipped at several Georgetown churches, with Mt. Zion Methodist as the most prominent—it is still an active congregation.

Known originally as The Little Ark, it became Mt. Zion in 1846, operating a school for the children of its congregants and serving as a stop on the Underground Railroad for slaves fleeing north. When its prosperity as a port city began to fade after the Civil War, Georgetown's wealthy whites quit the neighborhood, leaving behind a black community that, if it did not thrive economically, remained cohesive and vital well into the 20th century. By then, efforts to reclaim Georgetown, owing to a housing shortage that necessitated restoration, were in full swing. As whites slowly moved back to Georgetown's revitalized blocks, African Americans were forced out, many to nearby Prince George's County in Maryland, where real estate prices were more affordable. Today, few of Mt. Zion's members actually live in Georgetown—most travel from the suburbs for Sunday services.

Shown here in the 1930s, Mt. Zion Methodist Church began in 1816 when several black congregants, dissatisfied with their segregated status in the nearby Montgomery Street Church, split to form their own parish. After several ecclesiastical reconfigurations, that church grew to become Mt. Zion, which is now on the National Register of Historic Places.

## Georgetown's Mt. Zion Congregation

Students of the Children's Vacation Bible School pose in the churchyard at Mt. Zion Methodist Church in this photograph from the 1940s. The church began when several black congregants split to form their own parish, purchasing a lot on what is now 27th Street from Henry Foxall, a wealthy businessman. This early church, after several reconfigurations, plus a devastating fire that resulted in a rebuilding, became Mt. Zion.

In 1879, Mt. Zion Church purchased a parcel of land from another church to use as its burial ground. Earlier, the Female Union Band Society—a benevolent association of black women formed in 1842 for the purpose of providing burials for freed blacks—had purchased an adjacent parcel. Together they formed the Mt. Zion Cemetery, which served as final resting home for freed and enslaved blacks until 1950, when the city's Board of Health ordered internments to stop due to what, by then, had become an unkempt and unsafe burial ground. By the 1970s, the all-but-abandoned cemetery had become of interest to real estate developers, who were fended off in a 1975 court case by community activists arguing the cemetery's historic and cultural significance. In 1976, volunteers cleared the trash and restored the overgrown cemetery as part of activities associated with the nation's bicentennial. Along with the church, the cemetery is also listed on the National Register of Historic Places.

# GEORGETOWN'S HISTORIC HOMES

With the country in crisis due to the Great Depression and then World War II, Washington saw a steep increase in the number of federal workers who arrived from all over, though there was little affordable housing for them. Many of the so-called New Dealers of the 1930s and '40s looked to Georgetown, with its Federal-style townhouses untouched after several decades and ripe for restoration. In many cases, the basic structures were still intact. A strict preservation code enacted since then has largely kept them as they were.

The tiny Old Stone House on M Street, built in 1765, is the city's oldest surviving structure, but there are others equally as historic. The Tudor Place on 31st Street, now open to the public, was designed by Capitol architect William Thornton and was once owned by Martha Washington's granddaughter. The Forrest-Marbury House, which dates from 1788, was first home to an early Georgetown mayor, then to Judge William Marbury, a last-minute pick by outgoing president John Adams. This appointment led to *Marbury v. Madison*, the first constitutional challenge decided by the Supreme Court. In the 1980s, the house fell into serious disrepair but was restored and is now the Embassy of Ukraine.

Other former residents of note include Alexander Graham Bell, who operated a laboratory on 35th Street; Robert Todd Lincoln, the president's son, who lived at 3014 N Street until his death in 1926; and John F. Kennedy, who had several Georgetown addresses before he moved to the White House.

## Georgetown's Oldest

The Old Stone House on M Street was built in 1765 by cabinetmaker Christopher Lehman and was one the first structures to be built in Georgetown. Today, it's considered Washington's oldest building. Like Lehman, who had both his home and workshop here, the Old Stone House served as both residence and studio to a long line of artisans during the 19th century. By 1950, the house was rundown, and its historic significance was all but lost. It served as the base of operations for a used car dealer who turned the back garden into a car lot. Fortunately, the National Park Service acquired the property circa 1953. They restored the house and transformed the former car lot into a garden oasis in the middle of otherwise-hectic Georgetown.

## Tudor Place

Tudor Place, seen above as it looked around 1902 and as it looks today at left, was once home to Martha Custis, granddaughter of Martha Washington, and her husband, Thomas Peter, son of a wealthy tobacco merchant. In 1805, they hired William Thornton, one of the first architects of the U.S. Capitol, to design their Georgetown home, which stayed in the Peter family until 1983. The Peters were prominent in the early life of the republic and entertained many notables in their home, including the Marquis de Lafayette, considered a celebrity owing to his support of the American cause that had helped General Washington win the Revolutionary War. The house contains several items that once belonged to George and Martha Washington, and its a five-acre garden contains many of the tulip poplars, American hollies, and boxwoods originally planted by Martha.

# COX'S ROW AND COOKE'S ROW

Until 1871, when Congress annexed it as part of the capital, Georgetown was a city separate from Washington, a commercial rather than a political center with a distinct character as exhibited in its blend of architectural styles. Above the waterfront, most of Georgetown was, and remains, residential. The area is a mix of Georgian mansions and Federal-style townhouses built by wealthy ship owners, merchants, and speculators, such as John Cox, who served in the War of 1812 and was later a mayor of Georgetown. The five row houses that make up Cox's Row, as it's known, occupy a stretch of elegant N Street. The homes date from 1817 and are considered the city's finest examples of the Federal style. In the years immediately following the Civil War, Georgetown saw the addition of more building styles, including the Italianate row of four exquisitely preserved homes on Q Street known as Cooke's Row. Henry Cooke was a financier, businessman, and Republican politico whose friendship with President Ulysses Grant won Cooke the appointment (after the merger of Georgetown with Washington) to the newly created post of governor of the District of Columbia.

Cox's Row runs along the north side of the 3300 block of N Street, with John Cox himself at one time occupying the house he built in 1805 at 34th and N streets.

The homes on Cooke's Row, shown here in the 1960s, are today among Georgetown's finest examples of the neighborhood's early Italianate architectural style. The Italianate style began in England in the 1840s and slowly moved to the United States, where it took on American elements. Typically, Italianate-style homes are tall in appearance, with two to four stories, and are symmetrical (mostly rectangular) in shape. They often have eaves that jut out, with decorative cornices (*right*) and/or tall, narrow windows with Roman arches (*above*).

# DUMBARTON OAKS

This was once the home of a couple so perfectly named—Mr. and Mrs. Robert Woods Bliss—that they commissioned no less a talent than Igor Stravinsky to compose a piece in celebration of their 30th wedding anniversary. The Concerto in E-Flat (Dumbarton Oaks) had its 1938 premiere in the Bliss's lavish Music Room, where six years later in 1944, representatives from the United States, the United Kingdom, the Soviet Union, and China met to discuss the peace initiative that would lead to the formation of the United Nations.

Mr. Bliss had once been an ambassador to Argentina, and when he and his wife Mildred bought the house in 1920, they saw it as the perfect repository for their extensive collection of Byzantine artifacts, including 12,000 Byzantine coins and their pre-Columbian art collection, all of which was housed in eight glass pavilions designed by Philip Johnson.

Mrs. Bliss, with help from landscape architect Beatrix Farrand, turned the grounds' ten barren acres into an Eden of terraced gardens, which a full-time crew of 12 continues to maintain. In 1940, the property was transferred to Harvard, Mr. Bliss's alma mater. However, the Blisses themselves continued to develop the institution, collection, and gardens until their deaths in the 1960s.

*Top:* By the time this photo was taken in September 1944, diplomat Robert Woods Bliss and his wife Mildred, heiress to a patent medicine formula, had given Dumbarton Oaks to Harvard University to establish a research institute for Byzantine studies. The house was built in 1801 by William Dorsey, a judicial appointee of Thomas Jefferson, on land originally named for an ancient Scottish landmark. *Bottom:* Much of the Bliss Byzantine collection dates from the early period of the founding of Constantinople in A.D. 330 and includes chalices and patens used in the celebration of the Mass, plus gold jewelry and textiles. Their pre-Columbian collection includes Aztec sculptures, carvings, and masks; ceremonial objects from the Olmec; Mayan works in jade and shell; works in gold from Costa Rica and Panama; and pottery and textiles from Peru. Today, Dumbarton Oaks is a prime resource for scholars at work in these fields.

## Garden of Delights

Landscape architect Beatrix Farrand's stylized mix of French-, Italian-, and English-style gardens features colorful combinations of perennials and annuals and broad- and thin-leafed shrubs and trees (*far right*) set off with pools, pavilions, statuaries (*near right*), garden gates, and other structures. For almost 30 years, Farrand oversaw the Blisses' gardens, the records of her labor of love a valuable resource for the current team of gardeners. Of the original acres, only 16 remain under cultivation, and these, along with the house, are owned by Harvard University. Ten of the original acres were sold to the Danish Embassy, with the remaining 27-acre Lower Garden left to return to its natural state. It is now a public park.

The Blisses hosted musical performances, lectures, and discussions in the Music Room at Dumbarton Oaks. Its design is Renaissance in style and features Flemish tapestries, a French mantelpiece, and murals in the corridor painted by American Allyn Cox. The room continues to serve as a venue for lectures and an ongoing concert series.

## Oak Hill Cemetery

A bust of John Howard Payne (*right*) graces the grounds of Oak Hill Cemetery in Georgetown. Payne, an actor and poet, was best known for penning the words to the song "Home, Sweet Home," which begins, "Be it ever so humble, there's no place like home!" Since his passing in 1852, Payne's home has been Oak Hill Cemetery in Georgetown (*above*), designed as a lovely mix of 19th-century romanticism and English horticultural sensibilities. The cemetery was established by William Corcoran, an influential banker who also founded the Corcoran Gallery of Art. The chapel is the work of James Renwick, architect of William Corcoran's original art gallery (the city's first), which is located across the street from the White House and is known today as the Renwick Gallery. Among the notables buried at Oak Hill: Uriah Forrest, a lieutenant colonel who served under General George Washington during the Revolutionary War; Edwin Stanton, Lincoln's Secretary of War; and Joseph Henry, the first Secretary of the Smithsonian.

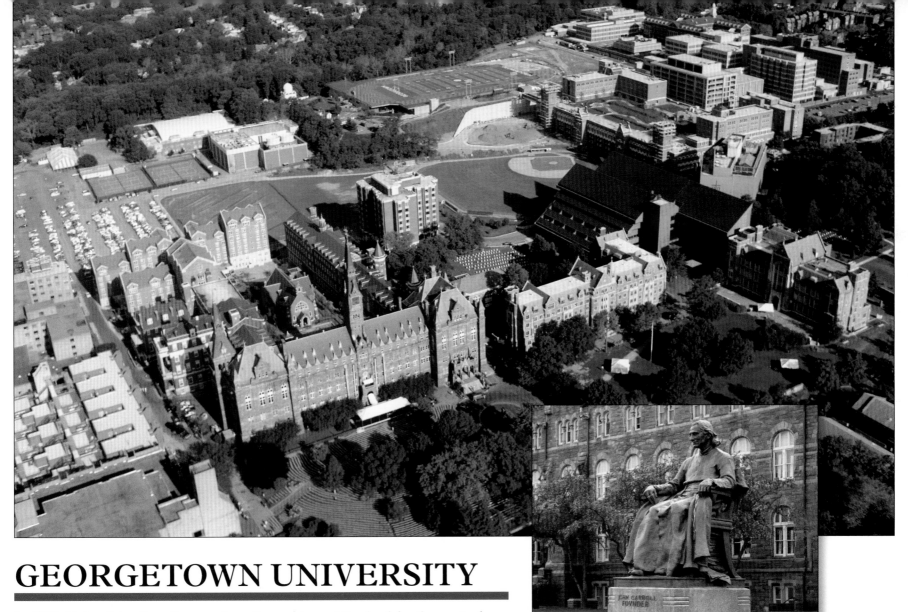

# GEORGETOWN UNIVERSITY

In 1789, Father John Carroll, a member of a prominent Maryland family, acquired a plot of land overlooking the Potomac. He opened an academy to provide a Catholic education in the rigorous Jesuit tradition to any male student, regardless of religious persuasion, who was up to the task. Carroll's academy grew into Georgetown University, the country's oldest Catholic college, and the institution of choice for two of George Washington's nephews. Between 1874 and 1882, when Jim Crow was in full swing and few African Americans rose to positions of public prominence, Georgetown had a black man as its president: Father Patrick F. Healy.

In its more than 200-year history, Georgetown has graduated many who have gone on to distinction, including President Bill Clinton, California First Lady Maria Shriver, playwright John Guare, and Supreme Court Justice Antonin Scalia.

*Top:* Georgetown University is the country's oldest Roman Catholic university and is comprised of four undergraduate schools. The 104-acre campus is located on the edge of Georgetown, its buildings a traditional mix of Gothic and Georgian with the Romanesque Healy Hall as its centerpiece. The building, now on the National Historic Register, was named for Father Patrick F. Healy, the university's president in the late 19th century and the first black man to hold such a post. *Bottom:* A statue of Jesuit Father John Carroll graces the campus of Georgetown University, which Carroll founded in 1789.

# New Wealth and Early Development

By the end of the 19th century, with the Civil War a memory and the nation's golden age before it, Washington shed its provincial image and began to emerge as the world's most important capital city. This importance derived mainly from the political power it had accrued in the process of keeping the Union together, but it also stemmed from another aspect—one that often accompanies power—and that was wealth.

Such as it was, Washington's 19th-century, prewar society had all but vanished—driven out by attrition and by sympathies that discouraged Confederate leanings. Filling the postwar void were members of the *nouveau riche,* such as Irish immigrant Thomas Walsh, who made a fortune mining gold, and Mary Foote Henderson, wife of a wealthy Missouri senator, whose success in real estate played a role in the city's early development. Washington, at last, was becoming a city of sophisticates, at least in those areas north of Georgetown such as Dupont Circle, Kalorama, Embassy Row, Woodley Park, and Cleveland Park, where residential development began in earnest.

### FROM THE GROUND UP

These areas were fit for development due to the concerns of infrastructure. To resemble a top-notch city, Washington had to lay the groundwork—installing sanitary sewers and water mains, paving and widening muddy roads, and then lighting and dressing up the roads with trees and parks.

A five-man band accompanies a Jazz-Age flapper in a performance in front of the polar bears' cage at the National Zoo.

*Opposite:* The Washington National Cathedral's 10-story-high nave and chancel—featuring inlaid marble and carved limestone arches—intersect the transepts and lead to the high altar, which is adorned with the Christ figure surrounded by the carved figures of 110 Christians.

The leader in this effort was Alexander "Boss" Shepherd, all but forgotten today, though in the 1870s, as the head of Public Works, he was responsible for almost single-handedly transforming Washington. Flamboyant and controversial, Shepherd's improvements tended, not surprisingly, to be more extensive in those areas where he and his wealthy friends had invested. Running well over his original budget, Shepherd eventually left the city in disgrace, though his legacy enabled Washington's rapid rise.

One of those areas to benefit most from Shepherd's touch was the Dupont Circle neighborhood, which had once been known ignobly as The Slashes, but which, by the turn of the century, was all but filled with fine mansions. Today, the circle itself, where Connecticut, New Hampshire, and Massachusetts avenues converge, is the fulcrum of a thriving and very hip commercial and residential area.

## EMBASSY ROW AND WASHINGTON'S DIPLOMATS

Along with attracting some of the nation's richest and most powerful, Washington, unlike any other city in the country, also drew a special class of foreign elites, ambassadors, and their embassy staffs, who hailed from almost every country in the world. These ranks of Washingtonians required no less than the best accommodations out of which to conduct the delicate business of diplomacy, and they secured these accommodations mainly along the length of Massachusetts Avenue known as Embassy Row. Many of the Embassy Row mansions had once been owned by the city's wealthiest—members of the set belonging to the Gilded Age, who, owing to reckless spending and the onset of the Depression, were eventually forced to sell. Many buyers of those grand homes turned out to be the governments of foreign countries on the lookout in the capital city for comparatively cheap embassy space.

## WOODLEY PARK AND CLEVELAND PARK

Of course, most Washingtonians had, and still have, lifestyles that, while comfortable, were far from lavish. In the early 20th century, these civil servants and members of the middle class flocked to newly created neighborhoods such as Woodley Park and Cleveland Park, where houses built and designed by developers and architects such as Harry Wardman and Waddy Wood were made with

Metrorail riders enter and exit the Dupont Circle Station via escalator.

Dupont Circle Station

style and quality. These new suburbs, once considered "out in the country," became connected by streetcar lines to downtown and to the government office buildings along Pennsylvania Avenue. With the National Zoo nearby, attracting not only tourists but local families, and the National Cathedral, well along in what turned out to be its 83 years of construction, the neighborhoods north of Georgetown, with their leafy streets and pleasant row houses, had the feel of a small town with all the advantages of a big city. Access to the Mall and the Smithsonian museums was a streetcar ride away. There was the Uptown Theater (an art deco gem of a movie theater), and all along Connecticut Avenue there were, and still are, plenty of shops and restaurants. Connecticut Avenue, the main thoroughfare, is almost all commercial now—some would argue too commercial—but the side streets have retained their original character, featuring blocks of stately homes in almost parklike settings, an extension of Rock Creek Park, Washington's premier green space.

## ADAMS MORGAN AND COLUMBIA HEIGHTS

Adams Morgan and Columbia Heights were developing, too, though these neighborhoods took different courses and came into their own later in the 20th century. Adams Morgan was a segregated community in the 1950s, but by the 1970s, it had become, and remains today, a successful mix of several ethnic groups. The area is popular with younger Washingtonians and a place where recent

immigrants can find vestiges of home in the groceries and shops along 18th Street and Columbia Road. Its evolution may have been gradual, but the changes seem to have taken firm root in Adams Morgan, while in nearby Columbia Heights, the turnaround has been more dramatic, with results that may be somewhat tenuous. Developers, with assistance from the city, recently transformed this blighted neighborhood, which sat neglected for nearly 40 years. It's a model of mixed-use, with housing available for all budgets, as well as

shopping and a Metrorail stop that makes for convenient city life. Unfortunately, the city's gangs still consider it a war zone, leaving the neighborhood's future in flux and wary residents, heavily invested in its success, clamoring for more police protection. It's too soon to predict how the neighborhood will fare in the long run, though there's enough at stake to put all bets on the side of the residents who, after all, want no different for themselves and their families than the generations of Washingtonians before them.

Garbed mannequins swing in an open-air shop in Adams Morgan.

# DUPONT CIRCLE

Since the 1960s, Dupont Circle has been the heart of the local cultural scene, a revolving registry of art galleries, trendy shops, funky cafés, and night spots. It's also the de facto hub of the city's gay and lesbian communities. Its grandest Beaux-Arts mansions are now private clubs, its art deco–style apartment buildings now home to the city's up-and-comers. It's where the stodginess that otherwise marks official Washington stops, and the beat goes on and on and on.

The circle, originally known as Pacific Circle, was once part of a grubby neighborhood called The Slashes, named for Slash Run, a stream used mainly to handle the discharge from several nearby slaughterhouses. In the 1870s, thanks to the intractable head of Public Works, Alexander "Boss" Shepherd, Slash Run was diverted into a sewer and buried beneath Connecticut Avenue, which Shepherd then had paved and widened. This made the area ripe for development, and soon, Washington's wealthiest were building their mansions there: homes with turrets and mansard roofs and elaborate gardens.

In 1882, the circle was rechristened in honor of Admiral Samuel F. DuPont, of the Delaware chemical family, who gave the Union its first naval victory of the Civil War when he captured Port Royal, South Carolina. But when he failed in his attempt to take Charleston, he was relieved of his command and later died in disgrace. His widow, Sophie, led the effort to revive the good admiral's name, culminating in congressional approval of funds for the circle's centerpiece fountain. It was designed by Daniel Chester French and Henry Bacon (collaborators on the Lincoln Memorial) and was dedicated in 1921.

As a neighborhood gathering spot, Dupont Circle has long been popular with everyone from chess players and dog walkers to street performers, political activists, and vendors. In the above photograph from 1923, an erstwhile balloon man makes a sale on the circle. Today, on a side street just off the circle, a farmers' market entices buyers with fresh fruits, vegetables, and cider (*left*).

Washingtonians stroll Dupont Circle's brick walkways in this colored postcard from the early 1900s. Originally called Pacific Circle, the park was renamed in honor of the Civil War hero Admiral Samuel F. DuPont whose statue, seen in the background, was replaced in 1921 with the circle's now iconic fountain.

*Above:* This elevated view shows Dupont Circle with its signature fountain in spring. Dupont Circle is formed by the convergence of Connecticut, New Hampshire, and Massachusetts avenues. Twenty-five feet beneath the circle lies 100,000 square feet of cavelike space, the remains of what had been the Dupont Circle trolley station—it was abandoned in 1962 after the city switched from streetcars to buses. *Right:* Daniel Chester French, sculptor of Dupont Circle's centerpiece fountain, was best known for his figure of Abraham Lincoln, which was installed within the memorial to the former president. To honor Samuel F. DuPont, French turned to the seafarer's art of celestial navigation for inspiration, erecting three classical figures representing the sea, the wind, and the stars, which connect the fountain's upper and lower basins.

## The Society of the Cincinnati

The Larz Anderson House, with its Italianate ballroom, as seen in these photographs from the mid-20th century, was one of Massachusetts Avenue's finest residences when it was completed in 1905. It served as home base for American diplomat Larz Anderson III, of a wealthy Cincinnati, Ohio, family, and his wife, Isabel, heiress of a Boston shipping magnate. The Andersons entertained presidents, kings, captains of industry, and even Sir Winston Churchill, in grand style here, at their winter quarters. The Andersons, who had several other residences, outfitted this home with a world-class collection of paintings, medieval tapestries, Asian art, ceramics, and furniture acquired during their travels. They were also civic-minded, contributing their time and money to several charities and other worthy pursuits, most notably the Society of the Cincinnati of which Larz was a devoted member. Several Continental army officers and French allies founded the society after the Revolutionary War to promote the ideals of liberty and good citizenship. In 1937, when Larz died, Isabel saw to the transfer of this home, and many of its furnishings, to the society for use as its headquarters. The society today has about 3,500 members made up of eligible descendants of American and French officers who served in the Revolutionary War.

The Blaine House, shown here in 1920, is Dupont Circle's oldest surviving mansion. Built in 1881, it was home to Maine Senator James G. Blaine, whose policies helped to define the early Republican Party as liberal and forward-thinking. Blaine also served in the House of Representatives and as Secretary of State and was widely respected for his intelligence, personal dynamism, and political savvy. But his implication in an illegal financial scheme, his contempt of civil service reform, and a streak of recklessness provided fodder for his enemies. Blaine died in

1893, and his home was sold to inventor/electricity pioneer George Westinghouse, who lived there from 1901 until his death in 1914. Today, the mansion serves as private law offices.

One of the city's best art galleries is in the former home of Duncan Phillips, heir to a Pittsburgh steelmaking fortune. In 1921, Phillips and his wife, Marjorie, converted two rooms of their home into a gallery to showcase what was quickly becoming the nation's premier collection of modern art. The Phillips Collection today holds close to 3,000 works, including those from Paul Klee, Mark Rothko, Georgia O'Keeffe, Georges Braque, and Pierre-Auguste Renoir, whose *Luncheon of the Boating Party* is the gallery's most popular and best known work.

Beer baron Christian Heurich owned a brick and brownstone Victorian, called the Brewmaster's Castle, on New Hampshire Avenue. Completed in 1894, it was considered the city's first fireproof residence due to its concrete and reinforced steel structure. Heurich also installed a bronze salamander—a creature that, in Greek mythology, protects against fire—on the tower's tip. Today, the home looks as it did when it was built. It has 31 rooms, including a music room (*top*) with a Steinway grand where quartets and other musical ensembles entertained the Heurich family and guests. Born in Germany, Heurich brought his brewmeister skills to Washington after the Civil War, where his Foggy Bottom brewery bottled Old Georgetown and Senate (whose early 20th-century promotional piece is shown at bottom) brands and made Heurich one of Washington's wealthiest citizens. By the 1950s, with the rise of nationally recognized beers, Heurich's sales flattened, forcing his business to close.

Customers crowd the outdoor café at Kramerbooks & Afterwords, a Dupont Circle institution since 1976. This independently operated bookstore and coffeehouse offers a small but choice selection of both titles and menu items. It serves as a hangout for night owls and early birds, and for those on a first date, it's *the* neighborhood meeting spot.

The Washington Metropolitan Area Transit Authority, or Metro, operates five lines over more than 100 miles of track in and around the city, with plans for further expansion into the suburbs. The stations, with their modern-styled vaulted ceilings of exposed concrete, were designed by architect Harry Weese. Washington's Metro is the nation's second busiest transit system, behind New York's. On January 20, 2009, Metro ferried more than a million people to and from Barack Obama's inauguration on the Mall.

# THE NAVAL OBSERVATORY AND THE VICE PRESIDENT'S HOME

Until 1977, the Vice President had no official residence but instead lived in private quarters of his choosing, an impractical arrangement given the cost and logistics of security. In 1974, Congress authorized the refurbishing of Number One Observatory Circle for vice-presidential use. Three years later, Walter Mondale, who served under President Jimmy Carter, moved in with his wife Joan.

The three-story, 9,100-square-foot Victorian was built in 1893 and was originally the home of the superintendent of the adjacent U.S. Naval Observatory until the Chief of Naval Operations, who loved the house, pulled rank and ordered the superintendent out in the 1920s.

The observatory itself was originally located in low-lying and industrial Foggy Bottom. Then, after 50 years, it moved to this hilly spot, which was rural in the 19th century and featured unobstructed views of the sky. One of the country's oldest scientific agencies, the observatory is the nation's official timekeeper and continues its work of charting Earth's rotation and the motion of other celestial bodies. The vice president's house is closed to the public, but visitors to the observatory can look through the 26-inch refractory telescope used in 1877 to discover two Martian moons.

*Above left:* The vice president and his family live in this three-story, Victorian-style home on the grounds of the U.S. Naval Observatory off Massachusetts Avenue near Embassy Row. *Above:* A skywatcher enjoys the magnified view at the Naval Observatory in this 1904 photograph.

# EMBASSY ROW

Most of the world's nearly 200 nations have embassies in Washington, the term "embassy" referring both to the chancery, where business is conducted, and to the separate residences of the ambassadors and staffs. Washington has almost 300 chanceries, both main and satellite offices, and an abundance of private residences—and all of this real estate is part of the territory of each of the nations. About 10,000 Washingtonians and foreign nationals work at the embassies, which pump about $400 million into the local economy. Most of the embassies are located west of 16th Street and north of the State Department in and around the upper stretch of Massachusetts Avenue, which is dubbed Embassy Row.

Washington's first Embassy Row was actually on 16th Street, where, in the early 20th century, the savvy wife of a wealthy Missouri senator built a dozen lavish mansions and apartments that she then sold or rented to several foreign countries. By then, the area around Dupont Circle was undergoing a real estate boom, triggered in part by the British, who had built the first embassy on Massachusetts Avenue, which, in turn, enticed several millionaires to move into the neighborhood.

In those pre-income tax days, the wealthy spent freely on their homes. By the Depression, however, many had gone bankrupt and were forced to sell on the cheap. Often, the first available buyers were foreign national governments.

Not all the embassies are located here—Canada's embassy is on Pennsylvania Avenue, Germany's in the Palisades, Switzerland's in Woodley Park, and Sweden's in Georgetown—but many, including the Turkish, Finnish, French, and Indonesian, remain anchors among the area's elegant blocks.

*The British Embassy*

This larger-than-life statue of Winston Churchill giving his famous "V for victory" salute stands outside the British Embassy along the busy stretch of Massachusetts Avenue known as Embassy Row. President Kennedy granted Churchill honorary American citizenship in 1963. As part of the 1966 ceremony that marked the event, a time capsule was buried beneath the statue, not to be unearthed until 2063.

The embassy of the Central African Republic of Cameroon occupies the former home of Christian Hauge, Norway's first minister to the United States, and his wife Louise. With its towers and candlesnuffer roof, this French-inspired home was designed by George Oakley Totten, one of Washington's top Beaux-Arts architects.

The French established their embassy in this chateau in the Kalorama neighborhood just off Embassy Row in 1936. The home was built in 1910 and was originally owned by an American mining magnate. In 1984, the French opened a larger and more modern chancery on Reservoir Road near Georgetown University, making this property the ambassador's exclusive residence.

## The Brazilian Ambassador's Residence

The Brazilian ambassador's residence was designed by classical architect John Russell Pope, who also designed the Jefferson Memorial. It is the former home of Cyrus McCormick, whose invention of the agricultural reaper led to the formation of International Harvester. When Brazil expanded its mission and opened an adjacent chancery in 1971, this building became the ambassador's residence.

## The Islamic Center of Washington

When the Turkish ambassador to the United States died in 1944, there was no mosque for his funeral. Desire for an Islamic place of worship somewhere in America spread, and Italian architect Mario Rossi, a convert to Islam, answered the call. The Islamic Center of Washington (*below*) was the largest place of Muslim worship in the Western Hemisphere when it opened. The Center includes the mosque, a library, and the minaret, which rises 160 feet. *Right:* The interior of the Islamic Center features this Egyptian chandelier, which weighs two tons. Other adornments include Persian carpets, stained glass from Iraq, and thousands of deep blue tiles from Turkey.

A few of the Muslim faithful gather to reflect and pray at the Islamic Center of Washington, three days after the September 11 attacks in 2001.

When it opened in 1957, the Islamic Center of Washington drew some 6,000 people to Friday prayers, though by the time this photograph was taken in 1988, that number had substantially increased. Here, worshippers overflow onto the sidewalk outside the mosque. Today, the Center serves as the cultural and spiritual Mecca to approximately 65,000 metropolitan-area Muslims.

The Indonesian embassy was originally the home of Irish immigrant Thomas Walsh, who made his fortune mining gold in Colorado.

# THE INDONESIAN EMBASSY AND THE HOPE DIAMOND

In the early 20th century, the city's grandest mansion was at 2020 Massachusetts Avenue, home of Irish immigrant Thomas Walsh, who struck it rich mining gold in Colorado. He won a senate seat from that state and arrived in Washington just in time to join the city's post–Civil War boom of *nouveau riche*. Washington was in full social swing in those turn-of-the-century days, and Walsh's 60-room mansion, with gold nuggets imbedded in its foyer floor, was the scene of high society's most lavish parties. Ostentation, however, eventually exacted its price.

Walsh's spoiled daughter, Evalyn, eloped with Ned McLean, playboy son of the wealthy owner of, among other things, *The Washington Post*, thus uniting two family fortunes that afforded the couple buying power that knew practically no bounds. Among their purchases was the alleged cursed Hope Diamond, a gem of unusual color and clarity. Supposedly stolen from its original setting in a sacred Hindu statue, it was said to be responsible for visiting upon all those who subsequently possessed it—including Marie Antoinette—all manner of calamity. In the case of Evalyn Walsh McLean, that calamity took the form of the deaths of her two children. At age nine, her son was struck and killed by a car as he crossed Wisconsin Avenue, and her daughter committed suicide. Dissolute and bankrupt, Ned McLean left Evalyn and died in an asylum. Evalyn died in 1947.

Walsh's magnificent Massachusetts Avenue mansion—which may have originally cost as much as $3 million—was sold to the Indonesian government in 1951 for a mere $335,000. It is now used as the Indonesian embassy.

Former Secretary of State Colin Powell offers condolences at the Indonesian embassy following the December 2004 tsunami that claimed more than 130,000 lives.

The 45.52-carat Hope Diamond, encircled by 16 white diamonds, is on permanent exhibit at the Smithsonian's National Museum of Natural History.

## ALEXANDER "BOSS" SHEPHERD

IN THE YEARS FOLLOWING THE CIVIL WAR, Washington was jammed with war-weary soldiers, political opportunists, and the newly emancipated—a tumbledown town in serious need of sprucing up. And Alexander "Boss" Shepherd was just the man to take on the challenge. A charismatic go-getter and unrelenting schmoozer, Shepherd had close, personal friend President Ulysses Grant appoint him to head the Board of Public Works, where, between 1871 and 1874, Shepherd oversaw the installation of hundreds of miles of sewer and gas lines, sidewalks, paved roads, water mains, and streetcar lines. He filled in the fetid canals, set aside parks, and planted tens of thousands of trees. Of course, Shepherd had help, most of it from his cronies and business associates, who profited with him (he owned the city's largest plumbing company and was director of four streetcar lines). In his campaign to transform Washington, Shepherd left nothing untouched, but his touch wasn't always gentle. When he felt that a meat and produce market called Northern Liberties Market (on the site of what is now Mt. Vernon Square) was competing unfavorably against the downtown Center Market that he backed, he ordered the demolition of Northern Liberties Market, during which a butcher, a boy, and a dog were crushed. Some called him "The Savior of Washington," but his ruthless tactics and profligate spending drew the ire of several members of Congress, who finally put a stop to his single-handedness when the tab for his beautification reached $26 million— much more than the budgeted $10 million. The abrupt end of his career threw Shepherd into personal bankruptcy, so he set off for Mexico with his wife and seven children. There, working his magic again, he turned a failing silver mine around, restoring his fortune. Unfortunately, his standing in Washington remained tarnished. He returned twice, to lukewarm receptions. By the time he died of appendicitis in 1902, he was all but forgotten, though his name has been revived of late. A statue of Shepherd, dedicated in 1909 but mothballed in the 1980s, was recently reinstalled in front of the Wilson Building, the District government's headquarters.

# ROCK CREEK PARK

The 19th century's Industrial Revolution, which resulted in the crowding and polluting of so many cities, also fed a counter movement in America that favored green spaces and public parks. The foremost champion of these areas was Frederick Law Olmsted Sr., perhaps best known for his design of New York's Central Park.

Frederick Law Olmsted Jr., continued his father's "city beautiful" work into the 20th century, notably in Washington, where he teamed with the McMillan Commission (responsible for so many of the improvements on the Mall and elsewhere) to officially make Rock Creek Park part of the city's park system in 1919.

More of a scenic reserve than a landscaped park, with its wooded slopes and craggy ravines, Rock Creek's land had once been privately held and was the site of several milling operations until the mid-19th century, at which point it was acquired by the federal government. Preservation efforts backed by congressional decree have saved these 1,754 pristine acres from the suburbanization that consumed areas adjacent to the park in the decades after the Civil War. At roughly four miles long and about a mile wide, the park, now under the aegis of the National Park Service, features trails for hiking and biking, a stable and riding center, an amphitheater, tennis courts, and golf links.

*Above:* Peirce Mill, seen here in a 1917 photograph, was built in the 1820s and was a working mill until the National Park Service acquired it from the Peirce family in the 1890s during the establishment of Rock Creek Park. Along with several other water-powered mills, there were also two large mansions and dozens of smaller dwellings occupied by immigrant and African American tenant farmers on the acreage set aside for the park. Recent archaeological digs have unearthed evidence showing that Native Americans had been encamped here as far back as 2500 B.C. *Right:* Roller skaters go for a spin through Rock Creek Park on a warm January afternoon in 1933.

In the 1920s, when this photograph was taken, Rock Creek was one of the few places to cool off during Washington's torturously hot summers. The Potomac would have been murky at best, and no doubt polluted, owing to the industrial discharge at Georgetown. The beach at the Tidal Basin would have been segregated. But at Rock Creek, the locals, regardless of race, could wade unimpeded amid the rocks where the stream runs rapid south of Military Road.

A young rider and her guide follow the equestrian trail in Rock Creek Park. Along with stables, the park has a nature center and planetarium that are especially popular with children and families. There's also a tennis stadium, where every August, top players on the tournament circuit play in the Legg Mason Tennis Classic. The Carter Barron Amphitheater, named for one of Rock Creek's former commissioners, opened to park goers in 1950 and offers a summer schedule of concerts and free performances of Shakespeare's plays to enjoy under the stars.

This Indian head carved of sandstone is the work of Denver sculptor Alexander Phimister Proctor and is one of 29 that adorn the Q Street Bridge over Rock Creek Parkway.

# ADAMS MORGAN

Adams Morgan is the city's most culturally diverse neighborhood, drawing newcomers from around the world with a vibrant mix of exotic restaurants, specialty shops, bars, clubs, and galleries that, alas, open and close with regularity, depending on the owners' cash flow and immigration status. It's a smorgasbord of languages and customs, everything from Hispanic and Mediterranean to West African, Asian, French, and Italian, where rappers and jazz musicians, traditional dance troupes, jugglers, and acrobats perform on streets jammed with weekend shoppers and bar-hoppers. Every September,

Adams Morgan throws a giant street party, and it certainly has cause to celebrate.

During the years of segregation, this neighborhood, originally part of four adjacent neighborhoods, was strictly split along racial lines. Its residents sent their children to either the all-white John Quincy Adams elementary school or the all-black Thomas P. Morgan. After the Supreme Court ordered school desegregation, a citizens group was formed for the purpose of improving the schools and generally encouraging more neighborliness. By the 1960s, the group, which

had taken its name from the two schools, had begun to turn things around. As the neighborhood came into its own, it adopted the name for itself, and by the 1970s and '80s, it had become a welcoming place for people of all cultures.

However, Adams Morgan has become a victim of its own success. Rising real estate prices, which have put it out of reach of many immigrants and long-time residents, and a rise in violent crime, owing in part to the increase in the number of taverns, have made the area somewhat less desirable.

The Duke Ellington Bridge crosses Rock Creek Park and links the Woodley Park and Adams Morgan neighborhoods. Originally named the Calvert Street Bridge, it features art deco–style bas-relief panels that were designed by Leon Hermant, who took transportation as his theme. The panel above pays homage to the steam engine. The bridge (*left*) was completed in 1935. It was renamed for famous band leader and native son Duke Ellington in 1974, following his death.

A mural of a red-headed woman marks popular Madam's Organ, the best known of the dozen or so bars and clubs along a lively two-block stretch of 18th Street in Adams Morgan. Club owner Bill Dugan commissioned artist Charlie Hababananda to paint the mural, which features the club's name and address along the décolletage, in the 1990s. After Hababananda finished, the city promptly fined Dugan for unauthorized advertising. Dugan won his case when he successfully argued that his mural was actually art. Since then, murals have become so popular and widely accepted that, in 2007, the city began Murals DC, a publicly funded program in which experienced artists partner with the young and aspiring to create outdoor works that reflect the culture and history of Washington's neighborhoods.

A mix of architectural styles marks 18th Street, the colorful heart of Adams Morgan.

The sidewalk display outside the Tibet Shop offers woven jars and bags for sale. Adams Morgan prides itself on its eclectic mix of specialty shops, trendy cafés and bars, and ethnic grocery stores.

# COLUMBIA HEIGHTS

A billion dollars worth of reinvestment has turned Columbia Heights, a once-fringe neighborhood, into a handsome mix of affordable apartments, condos, groceries, restaurants, and discount retailers.

Left blighted for almost 40 years after the arson and looting that followed the assassination of Martin Luther King Jr., the neighborhood was finally turned around as a result of a late 20th-century development scheme hatched by the city and several developers. After the riots, the city sold the vacant lots it acquired by eminent domain to developers at very reasonable prices. In exchange, the city was promised that the developers' plans would be inclusive, inviting a mix of residents who could walk to the grocery and other shops and enjoy sit-down meals at reasonably priced restaurants. The fact that Metrorail, the city's subway, had a Columbia Heights stop sweetened the deal.

And the developers delivered. Less than ten years after work began, at what *The Washington Post* reported in the spring of 2008 as "whiplash speed," Columbia Heights is hardly recognizable. With its 500,000-square-foot retail center; its theaters and restaurants; its rental units, some of them subsidized; and its affordable condos, it's a brand new city within the city—which may be part of the problem. Not everyone is on board when it comes to the neighborhood's rebirth, especially rival gangs for whom Columbia Heights remains a battleground. Despite increased police presence, there have been several shootings here, some of them fatal and many of them occurring on busy streets in broad daylight. In June 2009, rival gangs staged an afternoon gunfight at the Metro station in the middle of rush hour, critically wounding two, one of whom was an innocent bystander.

*Top:* These residences were constructed around 1890 in the Columbia Heights neighborhood, which, at that time, was considered a distant suburb. By the 1930s, development had transformed the open spaces into blocks of affordable, well-built brick row houses. But during the shift to the suburbs following World War II, Columbia Heights fell into decline. Finally, in 2000, the neighborhood began to turn around, and its revitalization is now complete. *Bottom:* Columbia Heights neighbors gather on the grounds of Cardozo High School during the 2007 4th of July celebrations to watch the fireworks over the Washington Monument.

This cool, cascading fountain is the centerpiece at Meridian Hill Park, where the French- and Italian-inspired gardens also feature statues of 15th-century French saint and hero Joan of Arc and 14th-century Italian poet Dante Alighieri.

# MERIDIAN HILL PARK

Meridian Hill is a testament to the power of what citizens can do when they're motivated and band together. This is what several local residents did in the 1990s after another park murder—this one of a teenager—left them shaken and angry. The 12-acre, classically inspired park, with its once-cascading fountain and impressive statuary, was by then a ruin—a hangout for drug dealers and criminals. Thus, the Friends of Meridian Hill began a nighttime patrol and clean-up effort. After a decade's work, with assistance from the National Park Service, they restored the park to its intended glory.

Called Meridian Hill because it's on the city's longitudinal line, the area was the site of Columbia College, which became George Washington University (now in Foggy Bottom). During the Civil War, Union troops camped here. By the 1880s, Mary Henderson, wife of a wealthy Missouri senator, had built a Romanesque mansion nearby and had a development plan involving the park and a dozen more fabulous homes and apartments around it. She rented these spaces to foreign legations and others of wealth. In 1910, the federal government bought the park land from Henderson, with plans to

develop it following the design of George Burnap, a landscape architect who drew his inspiration from French and Italian gardens. Construction dragged on for the next 25 years and was never completed. In 1949, the Henderson "castle" was torn down. By the 1960s, the park, unofficially renamed Malcolm X Park for the assassinated black nationalist, had become overgrown and was unsafe. Today, thanks to the Friends, it's a jewel among the city's many parks, popular with picnicking families and used as a neighborhood venue for summertime concerts and theatrical performances.

# WOODLEY PARK AND CLEVELAND PARK

Connecticut Avenue is the main thoroughfare in Woodley Park, a neighborhood that takes its name from the Woodley estate, which was the early 19th-century home of Philip Barton Key, a congressman and an uncle of Francis Scott Key (author of "The Star-Spangled Banner"). As the city's population grew after the Civil War, Woodley Park became prime for development, which started in earnest in the early 20th century. Affordable quality was the hallmark of many of the homes constructed by builder-developer Harry Wardman and others, and soon, Woodley Park became the neighborhood of choice for Washington's expanding civil service class. By the 1950s, Key's estate had become a school, and the neighborhood's two grand hotels were attracting not only upscale visitors but also some of the city's notables, such as Socialite Perle Mesta and John F. Kennedy. Although the neighborhood has become more congested, owing in part to the over-commercialization of Connecticut Avenue and the many tourists who rely on the neighborhood's Metro station to get to the nearby National Zoo, Woodley Park has retained its homey but urban feel.

Next to Woodley Park is Cleveland Park, a neighborhood many of Washington's 19th-century well-to-do called home, including Gardiner Greene Hubbard, first president of the National Geographic Society, and President Grover Cleveland, who gave the neighborhood its name. By the early 20th century, as Washington's population increased, Cleveland Park's suburbanization began, with most of the construction completed by 1930. The mix of Queen Anne-, Prairie-, and Colonial-style homes reflected the eclectic sensibilities of the era and were only enhanced when, later, the work of more modern architects such as Waddy Wood (with his Mission Revival style) and I. M. Pei (perhaps best known as the architect of the National Gallery of Art's East Wing) added to the pleasing mix.

*Above:* Secret Service agents scramble to shield President Ronald Reagan during the attempt on his life on March 30, 1981. The president had gone to the Washington Hilton Hotel in Woodley Park to address a gathering of labor leaders and was shot as he exited by John Hinckley, a deranged young man from Texas. The president suffered serious damage to his lung, but eventually made a full recovery. Hinckley was found not guilty by reason of insanity and has since remained confined to St. Elizabeths Hospital, a Washington psychiatric facility. *Left:* News of the attempt on the president's life made instant headlines across the country and around the world.

Portrait artist John Bailey painted this Marilyn Monroe mural on the side of Salon Roi, an upscale beauty shop in Woodley Park, in 1980 to commemorate salon owner Roi Barnard's 40th birthday. The portrait has since become a minor Washington landmark and has been reprinted on t-shirts and postcards.

# NATIONAL ZOOLOGICAL PARK

The National Zoo was established by congressional decree in 1889 and was officially absorbed into the Smithsonian Institution, of which it is still a part, the following year. Frederick Law Olmsted Jr., the nation's foremost landscape architect at the time, laid out the zoo's 163 hilly acres where today some 2,400 animals are housed. Like most zoos, the National Zoo, in its early years, put the emphasis on the enjoyment of visitors over the well-being of the animals—it did not even hire a full-time veterinarian until the mid-1950s. But as sensibilities shifted and more enlightened thinking took hold, the zoo shifted its focus and expanded its mission. In 1975, it established a 3,200-acre Conservation and Research Center in Front Royal, Virginia, a training ground for zoo professionals and a refuge for rare and endangered species in the mountains two hours west of Washington.

Thanks to Friends of the National Zoo, or FONZ, a nonprofit group established in 1958, the zoo's finances were assured as over the decades it acquired more animals and expanded its operations. FONZ's nationwide membership has since grown to 40,000, and its hands-on team of 1,000 local volunteers assist visitors and offer educational programs to teachers and students.

*Top:* Visitors stand before the cages at the National Zoo, hoping for a glimpse of a bear or two. The National Zoo was still a modest operation when this photograph was taken in the 1920s. *Bottom:* The sign marking the entrance to the National Zoological Park has long been a Connecticut Avenue landmark.

## Animals at the Zoo

Kiko, a young male orangutan, wows the crowd below as he swings hand-over-hand along the Zoo's Orangutan Transport System, or O Line (*left*). The O Line consists of eight 50-foot towers connected by 490 feet of plastic-coated steel cable that links the exhibit space to the orangutans' home, allowing the six orangutans to come and go as they please. *Above:* Giant panda Tai Shan digs into a cake made of bamboo and shredded beets during celebrations marking his fourth birthday in July 2009. In early 2010, Tai Shan was shipped to China to join the main breeding population there. His mother, Mei Xiang, and his father, Tian Tian, remain at the National Zoo (on loan from the Peoples' Republic). The pandas are the focus of a joint United States–China research and breeding project geared toward preserving this endangered species. Today, fewer than 1,600 pandas survive in their native Chinese bamboo forests. Of the 2,400 animals housed at the National Zoo, the pandas draw the most visitors.

# WASHINGTON NATIONAL CATHEDRAL

President Teddy Roosevelt laid the cornerstone of the National Cathedral, known officially as the Cathedral Church of Saint Peter and Saint Paul, in 1907, using the same silver trowel George Washington used to lay the U.S. Capitol's cornerstone in 1793. On September 29, 1990—83 years and tons of Indiana limestone later—one of the world's largest ecclesiastical buildings was finally complete.

This medieval-style marvel cost $65 million, all of the funds raised privately, and features 112 gargoyles, 231 glass windows, and more than a few flying buttresses. It occupies land once owned by Joseph Nourse, who arrived from England in the 18th century and built an estate he called Mount Saint Alban, after his Hertfordshire birthplace. English though its roots may be, the National Cathedral is all about the United States. George Washington himself envisioned such a cathedral when he prevailed upon original city planner Pierre L'Enfant to include it in his dream for the city. Even so, more than a century passed before Congress gave its blessing, in the form of a charter granted in 1893. Fourteen years later, construction finally began.

The cathedral is officially the headquarters of the Episcopal Diocese of Washington, but its ecumenical policy makes it a sanctuary for all believers, Christian and otherwise.

More than 150 notables are interred here, including President Woodrow Wilson and Helen Keller. Presidents Dwight D. Eisenhower, Ronald Reagan, and Gerald Ford each had their state funerals here, and on March 31, 1968, just five days before he was assassinated, Dr. Martin Luther King Jr. preached his last Sunday sermon from the cathedral's pulpit.

*Opposite:* Work on the National Cathedral, shown with scaffolding in place, was still more than 20 years away from completion in 1969. With its emphasis on the collective national spirit, the cathedral has been the site of historic events, including an official service of thanksgiving at the end of World War I, special monthly services in honor of U.S. armed forces during World War II, and a National Day of Prayer and Remembrance after the attacks of September 11, 2001. *Below:* The Washington National Cathedral is made almost entirely of Indiana limestone, erected in the stone-on-stone method of the great Gothic cathedrals. Unlike the more traditional Gothic cathedral with its emphasis on death and judgment, the overall theme for the west facade, seen here, is more hopeful. The areas above the three main doors, or portals, feature carvings depicting Creation. The cathedral's rose window is the facade's centerpiece, made of 10,500 pieces of glass. Above the rose window, between the two towers, is the Pilgrim Observation Gallery, offering a breathtaking view of Washington.

Every year, nearly 750,000 million people visit the National Cathedral for Sunday services, musical performances, lectures, and other events. Above, in May 1995, they are gathering for Sunday services. The Cathedral, due to its designation as our National House of Prayer, offers a spiritual home to all. Faithful followers of both rabbis and imams have gathered at the Cathedral for worship, as have those who adhere to the teachings of His Holiness the Dalai Lama, who appeared here before a capacity crowd in 2003.

A rooftop view of the National Cathedral shows the Gloria in Excelsis Tower against the eastern sky. The tower rises 300 feet and is equipped with two full sets of bells. The row of flying buttresses connects the cathedral's roof to the parapet, thus supporting the building by transferring the weight and forming bays for the artful placement of the stained-glass windows.

This gargoyle, one of 112, is part of the guttering system at the National Cathedral. Often carved as fantasy figures and human caricatures, gargoyles carry rainwater away from the building by way of pipes fitted into their mouths. Other figures, known as grotesques, deflect water by bouncing it off their heads or other surfaces. Often whimsical and sometimes wry, the cathedral's gargoyles and grotesques include devils, bears, donkeys, dragons, dogs, snakes, and even Darth Vader, the villainous *Star Wars* character.

The Washington National Cathedral has 231 stained glass windows, including these depicting the life of Jesus. The cathedral's most famous is the so-called Space Window, which commemorates the 1969 lunar landing and has a chip of moon rock that the astronauts brought back embedded within it. Other windows depict the lives of George and Martha Washington, Robert E. Lee, Abraham Lincoln, the adventures of Lewis and Clark as they trekked westward across the continent, and the events of World War II.

## Crypt of Woodrow Wilson

President Woodrow Wilson is one of the 220 people interred in Washington National Cathedral, with his crypt, shown here, located in a bay named for him. Wilson, born in 1856 in the mountain town of Staunton, Virginia, served as the nation's 28th president and was the second to win the Nobel Peace Prize (Teddy Roosevelt was the first) for his efforts to establish world peace in the wake of World War I. Wilson's "Fourteen Points" speech set the terms for his vision of lasting peace and the formation of the League of Nations, forerunner of the United Nations, but failed to sustain that vision in a substantive way. As some historians have argued, the limitations and impracticalities of that ideal led, less than two decades later, to the outbreak of World War II. His dream unrealized, Wilson died in 1924 of complications from a stroke.

# HILLWOOD ESTATE

Hillwood is the former home of Marjorie Merriweather Post, heiress to the Post Cereal fortune, who married four times. Her third husband, Joseph E. Davies, was ambassador to the Soviet Union in the 1930s. Mrs. Post, as she chose to call herself after the last of her divorces, had always been a serious collector of French decorative arts, but while stationed with Davies in Moscow, she also developed an interest in Russian liturgical art, which soon became her passion. The Soviets, gearing up for industrialization and in need of cold hard cash, sold many of their treasures to Mrs. Post, who was more than happy to have them.

In 1955, she bought Hillwood, built in the 1920s and known originally as Arbremont. Mrs. Post expanded it to accommodate her collections, a complementary mix of Rococo French and Imperial Russian, and in the Icon Room, she set on display some 400 icons, chalices, and other treasures, including creations by Carl Faberge, the celebrated jeweler to the Russian czars.

Hillwood is set on 13 acres and is best viewed in spring, when Mrs. Post's gardens, especially the azaleas, are in full bloom. Mrs. Post died in 1973.

*Above:* Hillwood, tucked on a leafy lane off busy Connecticut Avenue, was home to Marjorie Merriweather Post from 1955 until her death in 1973. The home, which sits on 25 acres and overlooks Rock Creek Park, was built in the 1920s. By the time this photograph was taken in 1969, Mrs. Post had transformed it substantially, with the intention that Hillwood serve not only as a gracious home perfect for entertaining but also as a museum to showcase her French and Russian art collections. *Right:* Mrs. Post loved dogs, lavishing them with such canine accoutrements as this canopied bed. Here she tends to Scampi, her schnauzer, in this photograph taken in 1964. Scampi is buried, along with his mistress's other pooches, at Hillwood's pet cemetery.

The Japanese Garden at Mrs. Post's Hillwood home is set off with a traditional granite lantern and a bridge over a cascading stream. Landscape architect Shogo Myaida designed this garden for Mrs. Post in the 1950s, combining plant materials native to Japan with azaleas, Colorado blue spruce, and other American plants. In addition to this garden and the Rose Garden, the Hillwood grounds also have a formal French parterre; an English garden walk known as the Friendship Walk; the wooded Four Seasons Overlook; the crescent-shape Lunar Lawn, where Mrs. Post hosted many outdoor receptions; a putting green; a Russian dacha surrounded by rhododendrons and azaleas; and a cutting garden and greenhouse.

## Russian Art at Hillwood

Along with several icons, chalices, vestments, and other liturgical objects, Mrs. Post's extensive Russian art collection includes two Imperial Easter Eggs crafted by Carl Faberge. The eggs were gifts of Nicholas II, the last czar, to his mother, Maria Fedorovna. The custom of presenting elaborately decorated eggs at Easter began in 1885 with Nicholas's father, Alexander III, and continued until the fall of the Romanovs in 1917 by which time Faberge had produced 50 of his fabulously jeweled eggs. This egg, known as the Catherine-the-Great egg, is made of gold and enamel and features cherubs, musical instruments, and depictions of the arts and sciences. Inside the egg was once a miniature figure of the empress, a patron of the arts and sciences, though the figure has been lost.

# Washington and the Future

If political power and wealth have been the overriding forces behind the emergence of "official" Washington and the city's thriving neighborhoods west of the Capitol, then what has defined the neighborhoods from 16th Street east to the Anacostia has largely been struggle.

These are the neighborhoods where race and poverty are linked, as seen in the crime-ridden streets. One in five Washingtonians lives below the poverty line and almost all are African American. So are many of the city's murder victims. After his 18-year-old friend was gunned down outside the Anacostia Metro station, a witness told the writer of a July 2009 *Washington Post* column, "It was a typical day in Southeast. You get shot at."

How Washington confronts this reality as it pushes itself forward through the 21st century is closely tied to development plans either under way now or in the formulation stages. These are sweeping plans that call for the wholesale transformation of some of the city's grittier neighborhoods and the building

of new neighborhoods where none existed before. The construction will go on for decades, with the cost at $12 billion thus far and likely to go higher. Washington is still a comparatively young city, younger than other world capitals such as Paris or London, and is still evolving as it works to define itself as more than just a city of monuments and government.

### THE BLACK MIDDLE CLASS

In the 1930s, the newly created Alley Dwelling Authority, empowered by Congress, surveyed Washington's blighted blocks and back alleys and condemned hundreds of dilapidated buildings. It was their attempt to remake a city in which thousands of homes, most of them occupied by African American families,

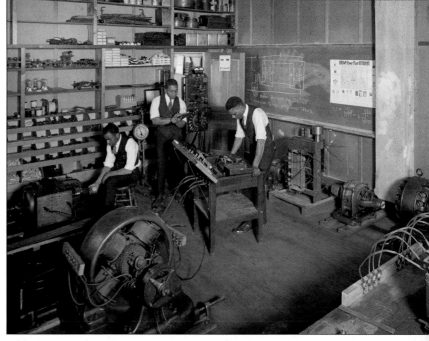

Howard University students in electrical engineering focus on their work in this photograph taken in 1915.

This early 20th-century photograph was taken not long after the Franciscan Monastery was completed. The church and friary dominate a hilltop in the Brookland section, which was then considered rural, where the brothers operated a small farm to sustain themselves. Today, with the addition of a fully equipped banquet hall, the monastery offers the perfect setting for weddings and other gatherings.

had no running water. By the 1950s and '60s, a new wave of so-called urban renewal turned what had been stable, if poor, black neighborhoods in Southwest and along its waterfront into warrens of new federal office buildings with highways dividing neighborhoods and public housing pushed to the fringes. Despite their successes, these programs left no doubt that their chief effect was the displacement of much of the city's black population, something that critics charge had been their true purpose.

After the Civil War, many African Americans migrating from the South chose Washington, where the Freedmen's Bureau offered assistance to former slaves and where there was a reasonable chance at a government job. However, Washington was locked in the grip of the Jim Crow era. Though the federal government provided employment, African Americans were consigned to low-level and custodial jobs. Segregation notwithstanding, Washington's small, black professional middle class managed to flourish and make a lasting mark on the city and its history. Young men and women educated at Howard University established themselves in such upscale neighborhoods as Logan Circle and LeDroit Park, where the tenor of cultural and intellectual life transcended Jim Crow. Even more modest communities such as Barry Farm in Anacostia, established in 1867 by the Freedmen's Bureau, fostered a close sense of community, with its early success contingent on each householder's sweat equity and sense of pride. Unfortunately, today Barry Farm has become run-down and is part of the scheme for renewal. Into the mid-20th century, U Street was also making its mark as the center of Washington nightlife for both blacks and whites. Its jazz clubs were popular with New Dealers of the 1930s and '40s and drew only the top black perform-

A Monarch butterfly aims for a landing at the Kenilworth Aquatic Gardens.

ers, including native Washingtonian Edward "Duke" Ellington.

## THE RIOTS OF 1968

Segregation, though, still ruled the day. In 1960, roughly half the city's 764,000 citizens were African American, yet none of them could so much as set foot in department stores such as Woodward & Lothrop or Garfinckel's or sit down to a meal at a good restaurant. Other stores would sell to blacks but not hire them. Washington's New Negro Alliance and other organizations had been pushing against discrimination since the 1930s, but their advances had been few and had done little to mitigate mounting frustrations. Then came the Civil Rights Movement, and in 1963, Martin Luther King Jr.'s appearance before an audience of 250,000 in front of the Lincoln Memorial. If his "I Have a Dream" speech raised hopes, those hopes were dashed less than five years later when, on the night of King's assassination, Washington erupted in a three-day rioting spree. It took 13 lives and caused a then-staggering $27 million in damage; Washington, 40 years later, is only just now recovering.

## FROM RUIN TO REBIRTH

So far, the U Street corridor, where the rioting began, has been the city's biggest comeback success, an area now filled with trendy shops and good restaurants. The corridor has become so popular that noise abatement has become an issue for owners of the neighborhood's new and pricey condos. Along with the waterfronts of Southwest and Southeast, the

Georgia Avenue corridor, once blighted by drugs, will also be getting a facelift, though the closing of the landmark Walter Reed Medical Center, scheduled for 2011, leaves its fate somewhat uncertain. During the last decade, a spirit of renewal has completely overtaken Washington; it shows no signs of letting up, though some of Washington's most beautiful and historic sites will be left untouched—sites such as the grand

Basilica and the peaceful Franciscan Monastery, part of the city's Catholic enclave known as "Little Rome." Once the transformation is complete, cherished havens such as the Kenilworth Aquatic Gardens and the National Arboretum will be more accessible to all and surrounded by revitalized and safe neighborhoods where crime is not a given and where getting shot at is no longer part of a typical day.

The Great Upper Church at the Basilica of the National Shrine of the Immaculate Conception is designed in the Romanesque-Byzantine style, a pleasing mix of arches and domes. The seven main domes are embellished with more than 75,000 square feet of tiles featuring mosaic scenes depicting the life of Jesus and other hallmarks of Catholic divinity. Nearly 400 feet long and 180 feet at its transepts, the Great Upper Church can hold as many as 6,000 worshippers. While the Shrine's Great Upper Church is a blend of the Roman and Byzantine, its Crypt Level is modeled after the catacombs built during the period of the early Christians in Rome and features a more modest and cavelike church.

# LOGAN CIRCLE

This circle at the intersection of Rhode Island and Vermont avenues was originally a triangle in L'Enfant's 1790 plan for the city. In the 1870s, Alexander "Boss" Shepherd, head of Public Works and responsible for the sweeping transformation of Washington after the Civil War, turned the triangle into Iowa Circle and ringed it with stylish Victorian homes for the city's well-to-do. By the turn of the 20th century, the wealthy had moved up and out to the areas around Meridian Hill, Kalorama, and Sheridan Circle.

In the 1930s, the circle was renamed for John A. Logan, a former Illinois senator and champion of the Union. By then, the area around it had become a vibrant middle-class African American neighborhood, home to teachers, doctors, civil rights lawyers, artists, and pastors. But in the 1960s, as residents left for the suburbs, Logan Circle fell into decline and became a neighborhood where drugs and crime took the lead for much of the next four decades. In 1990, in a run-down hotel room just a few blocks away at Thomas Circle, former mayor Marion Barry made international headlines when he was caught on tape smoking crack cocaine in an FBI sting operation, an incident that put new focus on what life in the "other" Washington—the one that doesn't involve power brokering and excessive wealth—was becoming. But those days are all in the past. City leaders working with developers have slowly turned the area around, replacing former crack houses with new condos and shops and restoring many of Logan Circle's fine old Victorians to their former glory.

The Mary McLeod Bethune Council Home was once the headquarters of the National Council of Negro Women, founded by Bethune in 1935, and is now operated by the National Park Service as a museum dedicated to the memory of this educator and civil rights activist. Bethune (1875–1955) was a child of former slaves and rose to become a member of Franklin Roosevelt's inner circle, advising him during the Depression and World War II. Her former home contains the nation's largest National Archives for Black Women's History.

*Above:* Logan Circle's original Victorian gems, shown here in the 1890s, have since been upgraded. The Logan Circle neighborhood, with its 135 late Victorian- and Richardsonian-style townhouses, was listed on the National Register of Historic Places in 1972, although the grand old homes were crumbling by then. By the 1990s, the high cost of housing in the Washington metro area forced the return of a new middle class, buyers with more know-how and skill than cash, who reclaimed once elegant Logan Circle and turned it around in little more than a decade.

# LeDROIT PARK

Named for LeDroit Langdon, a successful real estate broker, this neighborhood was developed in the 1870s. It was intended for white middle-class professionals and civil servants who had flocked to Washington after the Civil War and had settled other neighborhoods such as Columbia Heights and Brookland, near Catholic University. LeDroit Park's single-family homes and row houses were an eclectic mix of late Victorian styles—everything from Gothic Revival to Queen Anne—equipped with the latest amenities and set amid charming cottage-style gardens. Adjacent to historically black Howard University, LeDroit Park also had one other feature: It was surrounded by a fence and patrolled by guards, an early example of a so-called gated community whose purpose had little to do with safety and all to do with keeping out the African American students. One July day in 1888, several students tore down the fence, launching a bitter racial dispute that wasn't settled until the early 20th century, when whites began moving out. Between the two world wars, LeDroit Park developed as an upscale black neighborhood, home to luminaries such as poet Paul Laurence Dunbar and Benjamin Davis, America's first African American general. The troubled 1960s brought decline, but the neighborhood's affiliation with the university has boosted restoration efforts and secured its historic status.

*Right:* As Washington slowly came into its own as a world capital in the decades following the Civil War, late Victorian-style townhouses, such as these, were built to house the emerging civil servant and professional class. But by the 1950s, with the flight to the suburbs, many of these homes had begun to fall into disrepair, including those in and around LeDroit Park, Logan Circle, and the Shaw neighborhood, where crime and drugs contributed to physical decline and an overall atmosphere of despair. Revitalization—driven by a spirit of urban pioneering among private owners—has brought back many of these beauties, with their arched bay windows and finial-topped turrets.

## First Mayor

*First Mayor*

Former city mayor Walter E. Washington lived in this large corner house on T Street. The aptly named mayor was the first to serve in the post, elected after Congress granted Home Rule in 1973, which gave city residents a say in the workings of the local government but still no voting member in Congress. Mayor Washington, born in 1915, earned his law degree from Howard University and began his civil service career as a member of the city's housing authority. In 1961, he was appointed by President Kennedy to head the agency. In the era before Home Rule, Presidents Johnson and Nixon appointed Washington to serve as Mayor-Commissioner, as the city's top post was then called, though his executive privileges were limited. Washington was sworn into office as the city's first elected mayor on January 2, 1975, and served one term, after which he resumed his law practice. He died in 2003.

Into the 1950s, the main attraction on this stretch of U Street was the Lincoln Theatre, seen here not long after it opened in 1922. The Lincoln catered to an all-black clientele but fell into decline with desegregation as blacks gained access to other theaters and public places. It closed altogether after the 1968 riots. The Lincoln opened again in 1993 after an extensive restoration but still struggles financially.

# U STREET AND THE 1968 RIOTS

In the early to mid-20th century, U Street was known as "black Broadway," the epicenter of African American social and cultural life, a neighborhood filled with jazz clubs, restaurants, and theaters. There were also bakeries, print shops, hardware stores, and beauty shops in this lively commercial and residential area. By the 1960s, however, U Street and other traditionally black neighborhoods, such as those around 7th, 14th, and H streets, were mostly inhabited by an increasingly frustrated black underclass, left behind in the general migration to the suburbs to work the lowest paying jobs and live in rat-infested buildings. By the summer of 1967, African Americans in other cities such as

Detroit and Newark, suffering the same pressures, rioted to devastating effects.

On March 31, 1968, against the rising tide of unrest, Martin Luther King Jr., in what would be his last Sunday sermon, declared before a large congregation at Washington's National Cathedral, "The judgment of God is upon us today.... It is no longer a choice, my friends, between violence and nonviolence. It is either nonviolence or nonexistence." Four days later, on April 4, King was assassinated in Memphis. And at 9:25 P.M., the rioting on U Street began. The Peoples Drug Store at 14th and U was the rioters' first target. This incident triggered three

days of mayhem that spread to every quadrant of the city, leaving 13 dead and more than 1,000 injured and taking 13,600 federal troops to quell. When the smoke from more than 200 fires finally cleared, Washington, particularly its black neighborhoods, was in shambles. Rebuilding languished for three decades, the result of corruption and fiscal malfeasance. But by the 1990s, developers, eyeing Washington's vacant lots and enticed by the city's offer of tax incentives, began rebuilding the riot-savaged corridors. So far, U Street has been the most successful—so successful in fact, that more than 26,000 now call this once abandoned neighborhood home.

## The Riots of 1968

*Above left:* Bands of looters, as well as the simply curious, advance along a city street in the aftermath of the 1968 riots. Nearly 100 businesses closed or were destroyed. *Above right:* Two thousand paratroopers of the 82nd Airborne Division take their positions to assist National Guard units already on patrol in riot-torn Washington, while firefighters douse a blaze. Many fires were set by arsonists during the violence that erupted following Martin Luther King Jr.'s assassination. It took more than 13,000 federal troops occupying the city for 12 days to finally restore order. *Left:* This aerial view shows the still-smoldering buildings along H Street between 12th and 13th streets after fires claimed the neighborhood during the riots.

A mural on an exterior wall of Bohemian Caverns, one of U Street's original and legendary jazz clubs, features Miles Davis and Shirley Horn. All through the 1930s and '40s, Washington's café society gathered at clubs such as Club Caverns, as it was originally known, to hear such jazz greats as Duke Ellington, Billie Holiday, John Coltrane, Louis Armstrong, Ella Fitzgerald, and Billy Eckstine. The neighborhood, today known as Shaw or the U Street corridor, was to Washington what Harlem had once been to New York, an epicenter of black social and cultural life. In the early 1950s, Club Caverns changed its name to Crystal Caverns, then, in the late 1950s, to Bohemian Caverns. It remains the only survivor of that golden era, still booking jazz and R&B acts and attracting a new generation of music lovers.

## *The Duke*

This mural of jazz great Duke Ellington was painted in 1997 by G. Byron Peck; in 2004, it was placed on the side of the True Reformer Building, originally home to the black fraternal benevolent society known as the United Order of True Reformers, which offered banking and other financial services to its membership. The building, which also housed several shops, a supper club, and a vocational school, formed the commercial core of the U Street neighborhood well into the 20th century. The building also served as a dance hall, a gymnasium for boys, and a recruiting station during both world wars. It was in this hall that Duke Ellington, who grew up nearby, and his band gave one of their earliest performances.

In 1958, Mahaboob Ben Ali opened the Chili Bowl on U Street, still a thriving center of black life, serving his special concoction (a secret family recipe) atop hot dogs, hamburgers, and half-smokes. During the decades of neighborhood neglect, Ben's Chili Bowl managed to prosper, emerging as the centerpiece of a revitalized U Street. Bill Cosby is a regular here and has a posted sign declaring that he eats free. So does President Obama, whose name was added after he dropped in for lunch a few days before his inaugural. Although Ali died in 2009, his beloved eatery hasn't. It is now in the care of two of his three sons.

## EDWARD "DUKE" ELLINGTON

EDWARD "DUKE" ELLINGTON WAS BORN IN 1899 and grew up in the neighborhood now known as Shaw, just a few blocks away from the clubs and theaters that were once the heart of Washington's "black Broadway." His father, a butler and caterer and then a technician at the Navy Department, was known for his sophisticated bearing and impeccable dress, traits passed to his son, which helped him earn his royal nickname. Duke had a typical boy's passion for baseball, but he loved the piano more. A neighbor, who was a high-school music teacher, helped Duke develop his gift and put him on the path that would secure him as a legend. While working after school as a soda jerk, Duke composed his first piece, "The Soda Fountain Rag," and soon began sitting in with local bands booked at the Poodle Dog Café and other U Street clubs. Duke's Serenaders, as he called his first band, were soon headlining at True Reformers, a mutual aid society with a dance hall, at its U Street location.

By the 1920s, crowds both black and white flocked to hear Duke's Washingtonians. Popular though he was, Duke realized Washington was too small and that he had to head to New York, a wise move that landed him and his newer, much larger band a regular gig at Harlem's famed Cotton Club. A masterful arranger, Duke was also a prolific songwriter, composing more than 3,000 songs, including such standards as "Satin Doll," "Don't Get Around Much Anymore," and "Mood Indigo." In 1943, Duke played Carnegie Hall; he was the first non-classical musician booked there. In the years following World War II, however, with the rise of rock 'n' roll, Duke's popularity slipped. But his performance at the 1956 Newport Jazz Festival revived his stalled career, winning him a new generation of followers worldwide. Duke died at age 75 in 1974. The Calvert Street Bridge was renamed the Ellington Bridge in his honor by Washington, D.C., the city that also opened the Duke Ellington School of the Arts, a public school on R Street in Georgetown, which offers training to the city's most artistically gifted students.

# HOWARD UNIVERSITY AND FREEDMEN'S HOSPITAL

Howard University, which opened its doors in 1869 to only a handful of students, is the nation's oldest and most prestigious African American university, with a current enrollment of 11,000. It was named for General Oliver Otis Howard, head of the Freedmen's Bureau, which, after the Civil War, provided assistance to four million former slaves who were freed but impoverished, displaced, and uneducated. The university was substantially underwritten by the bureau in its early years but, oddly, did not have a black president until 1926. It did, however, have a number of distinguished black faculty members, among them John Mercer Langston, a Civil War hero and the son of a freed woman and her former white master. Langston became the first dean of the law school whose later alumni included Supreme Court Justice Thurgood Marshall, appointed by President Lyndon Johnson, and L. Douglas Wilder, who served Virginia as the nation's first black governor from 1990 to 1993. Langston Hughes, an influential poet of the Harlem Renaissance, was John Mercer Langston's great-nephew and namesake.

Aside from its top-notch law school, Howard University has one of the nation's best medical schools, which grew out of the original Freedmen's Hospital, established in 1862. In that year, the hospital administered to escaped slaves and other refugees in desperate need of medical attention after their arrival in Washington. Under the leadership of several notable black physicians—including Dr. Daniel Williams, who performed the first successful heart surgery at Chicago's Provident Hospital in 1893—the hospital's reputation grew. By the 1960s, however, its facilities were outmoded and in serious disrepair. In 1975, Freedmen's became Howard University Hospital, a modern complex on Georgia Avenue on the former site of Griffith Stadium.

*Left:* When this photograph of Old Main at Howard University was taken in the early 20th century, there were fewer than 1,700 students enrolled in the university's eight schools and colleges, none of which held national accreditation. But by 1960, Howard had ten fully accredited schools and 6,000 students, some of whom were candidates for PhD degrees. Old Main, constructed in 1867, was the university's first building. It was torn down in 1940, and Founders' Library was built in its place. *Above:* By 1946, when this photograph of students in a surgical theater was taken, Howard University's medical school was well on its way to establishing its top-notch reputation.

The campus of Howard University, shown in this aerial photograph, occupies more than 250 acres and is composed of 12 schools and colleges. It boasts more African American PhDs than any other university in the world. Famous alums include Pulitzer Prize–winning author Toni Morrison, opera singer Jessye Norman, actress and director Debbie Allen, two of Washington, D.C.'s mayors, and Supreme Court Justice Thurgood Marshall.

## Rock Creek Cemetery

Rock Creek Cemetery is the final resting place for many Washington notables. Visitors from all over the world come to see the cemetery's many monuments and sculptures, the most popular of which is a hooded and inscrutable figure that Washingtonians have come to call *Grief* (*above*). In order to assuage his grief over his wife Marian's death, Henry Adams (historian, journalist, and descendant of founder John Adams) commissioned sculptor Augustus Saint-Gaudens to create this funerary statue at the cemetery. Marian Hooper "Clover" Adams committed suicide in 1885.

# GEORGIA AVENUE

Originally a toll road when it opened in 1829, Georgia Avenue is the city's main north-south thoroughfare and the heart of a mixed-bag community on the threshold of revitalization. "The Avenue," as it's known to those who live along it, is a four-mile strip of beauty and barber-shops, liquor stores, mom-and-pop markets, thrift stores, rib joints, and bars that gradually give way to condos, townhouses, and sit-down restaurants—which some fear may displace Georgia Avenue's colorful history and ethnic flavor. Its surrounding neighborhoods are home to African and Caribbean immigrants and longtime black Washingtonians.

These residents remember Georgia Avenue institutions such as the La Savage Beauty Clinic, which catered to the smartest Howard University coeds in the 1940s and '50s and made a wealthy woman of the flamboyant Grace Savage, as well as the Temple of Freedom Under God, Church of God, from which exuberant evangelist Elder Lightfoot Solomon Michaux regularly broadcast his uplifting sermons to a national radio audience during the 1930s and '40s.

Georgia Avenue is the main link between middle-class Takoma Park in the north, working-class Petworth and Howard University in the south, the mix perhaps in part responsible for holding this community more or less together as the city endured the 1968 riots. But then came the drug epidemics of the 1970s and '80s, and Georgia Avenue emerged more than a little worse for wear and with a serious crime problem that still lingers. Redevelopment is sure to improve the neighborhood's fortunes, though one of the keys rests with the future of Walter Reed Army Medical Center, which will move from its present 113-acre site to Bethesda, Maryland, in 2011, leaving a considerable vacancy on The Avenue.

### Walter Reed Army Medical Center

Two Iraq War amputees aided by the latest in prosthetics demonstrate agility exercises at the Walter Reed Army Medical Center's Military Advanced Training Center. The Center opened in 2007 with a focus on rehabilitating war veterans who have lost limbs. The medical center was named for Major Walter Reed, an army physician during the Spanish-American War, whose study of tropical diseases, most notably yellow fever, led to the breakthrough discovery of the role mosquitoes play in transmission. The hospital opened in 1909, a single building with 80 beds. Today, Walter Reed serves thousands of military personnel and their families every day on its 65-building campus, which includes a ten-story hospital, recreational facilities, and several medical research labs. Walter Reed will be shuttered in 2011, its medical operations transferred to the National Naval Medical Center in nearby Bethesda, Maryland.

# CIVIL WAR FORTS

Five of the city's original Civil War forts—Forts Stanton, Davis, Dupont, Chaplin, and Mahan—are located in Anacostia, part of the 68-fort system of "Fort Circle Parks" so essential to the defense of Washington. Fort Dupont, now a popular park, was the largest, charged with guarding the bridge over the Anacostia River near the Washington Navy Yard. No battles were fought at the fort, and the earthworks are all that remain.

Although some of the war's most significant battles, such as Manassas, Antietam, and Gettysburg, were fought within a day's ride of the city, Washington itself was the site of only one attack, this on July 12, 1864, when Confederate General Jubal Early, in a desperate attempt to turn a losing tide, sent his exhausted troops to engage seasoned Union soldiers who repelled Early. Abraham Lincoln rode out to observe the action, only to be the target of a sharpshooter—the only president so far to be shot at in wartime.

As Anacostia undergoes development, the parks will be incorporated into a plan that expands the green spaces on the east side of the river and includes a foot and bike path linking the area to the Mall.

The barn shown in this 1944 photograph is located in Fort Dupont, one of 68 forts that encircled Washington during the Civil War. Soldiers garrisoned at Fort Dupont were charged with defending the 11th Street Bridge across the Anacostia River, near the Washington Navy Yard. Named for Union naval hero Samuel F. DuPont, of the famous Delaware chemical family, this fort was Washington's largest and was protected by a moat. Although the soldiers were never called into battle, the fort served as a safe haven for many runaway slaves on their way to freedom in the North. In the 1930s, the fort and 376 adjacent acres were made into a park, which today features several athletic fields and trails.

The Anacostia Community Museum, one of the Smithsonian Institution's museums, was founded in 1967 and offers exhibitions and educational programs that reflect the experience of Washington's African American community. Although its focus is primarily local, its collections include artifacts from other black communities both in this country and in West Africa. Its research facility includes family archives, photographs, diaries, public records, and other holdings, while its Museum Academy offers ongoing cultural programs for young students.

# THE LINCOLN COTTAGE

For more than a quarter of his presidency, Lincoln lived in this 34-room Gothic Revival home with his wife Mary Todd and youngest son Tad, commuting 45 minutes every day to the White House. In 1862, the Lincolns lost their 11-year-old son, Willie, to typhoid. This tragedy, combined with the horror of the Civil War and the misery of Washington in summer, with its heat and malaria and fetid water, forced the family's retreat to this cottage on the grounds of the Soldiers' Home (now called the U.S. Armed Forces Retirement Home). Aside from the respite that life at the cottage offered, what Lincoln saw on his daily commute may have helped to sharpen his convictions. The city itself had been the site of only one skirmish, but Washington was a scene of devastation, with its overrun hospitals, its encampments of runaway slaves, its wagonloads of wounded and exhausted soldiers, and its roaming bands of frustrated pro-Southern sympathizers. One morning during Lincoln's commute, a sniper shot off the President's hat.

That summer, while at the cottage, Lincoln crafted the Emancipation Proclamation, freeing all slaves by executive order, which he declared publicly in September, four days after the pivotal battle at Antietam in Maryland. Lincoln also spent his time at the cottage reading the Bible and Shakespeare and, of course, grieving Willie, whom Mary tried desperately to contact through the séances she held while she was there.

*Above right:* Shown here is the back porch of the Lincoln Cottage as it looked in the mid-20th century. The 34-room Gothic Revival-style home was built in 1842 and was the summer residence of Washington banker George Riggs. In 1851, Riggs sold the cottage and the surrounding 272 acres to the federal government for a retirement center for veterans. The campus has since grown but still serves the needs of retired military as the Armed Forces Retirement Home. During his presidency, Lincoln and his family used the cottage as a much-needed getaway from the White House, as did presidents James Buchanan, Rutherford B. Hayes, and Chester Arthur. *Right:* This photograph shows the front of the Lincoln Cottage as it appears today after a seven-year restoration that cost more than $15 million.

*Right:* The parlor at the Lincoln Cottage was restored to the way it appeared in the 1860s, when the president and his family lived at the cottage. *Below left:* A checkers table is set for a game in the library of the Lincoln Cottage where the president played the game with his son Tad. *Below right:* A bronze statue of President Lincoln and his horse stands on the grounds of the restored and recently reopened Lincoln Cottage. Between 1862 and 1864, the Lincolns spent much of their time at the cottage, the president making the daily three-mile commute to the White House by carriage or on horseback.

# THE BASILICA OF THE NATIONAL SHRINE OF THE IMMACULATE CONCEPTION

In 1990, this Catholic church (the largest in the Americas) was designated a basilica by Pope John Paul II. The term *basilica* is derived from the Latin word for a type of building in which government business was conducted. Christians also used this type of building for their worship services beginning in the fourth century. Today the papal designation is reserved for those churches of historic or cultural importance or those that have some special significance. The National Shrine is dedicated to the Virgin Mary and was deemed a basilica because of her role as Catholic Patroness of the United States.

In 1913, the adjacent Catholic University donated the three-acre parcel on which the basilica sits. Construction didn't begin until 1920 and continued in fits and starts until the basilica was finally completed in 1959. Every year, 500,000 people worship at the National Shrine's Crypt Church and its Great Upper Church.

The Basilica of the National Shrine of the Immaculate Conception was erected as a monument to Mary and is an intentional blend of Romanesque and Byzantine styles. The shrine, which ranks among the world's ten largest churches, was constructed entirely of stone, brick, and tile using traditional methods of support and requiring no structural steel. The Great Dome, the dominant Byzantine feature with its polychrome roof, is 108 feet in diameter. The campanile, or bell tower, rises 329 feet, making it one of the tallest structures in Washington. *Right: Christ in Majesty,* as this mosaic is known, is one of the world's largest mosaics of Jesus and dominates the north apse of the Great Upper Church at the Basilica of the National Shrine of the Immaculate Conception.

This chapel is one of 70 at the shrine and features Byzantine-style icons. In a truly catholic and all-American spirit, the shrine pays homage to every group, from the Irish to the Slovenian, to the Chinese to the Latin American—and more—in its chapels, which are decorated in the style reflective of each group.

## Red Mass

In 1942, the faithful gather for a Red Mass at one of the chapels on the campus of Catholic University. The Masses are traditionally offered for attorneys, judges, and others in the legal profession so that they may be guided by faith and act with deliberate justice. First offered in medieval Europe, the Red Mass is so called for the red vestments worn by the priest as a symbol of the Holy Spirit. One of the best known of the Red Masses is celebrated downtown at St. Matthew's Cathedral on Rhode Island Avenue on the Sunday before the Supreme Court convenes each October. In addition to many of the justices, the Mass also draws members of Congress and the Cabinet as well as other top officials and notable Washingtonians.

## Catholic University

The Catholic University of America was founded by the U.S. Catholic bishops whose aim was to incorporate into the Catholic educational system the research and learning approaches of the modern university. With Pope Leo XIII's blessing, the university opened its doors in 1889. Catholic U's sprawling 193-acre campus is located in the Brookland neighborhood, immediately adjacent to the Basilica of the National Shrine of the Immaculate Conception.

# THE FRANCISCAN MONASTERY

At the end of the 19th century, two Catholic priests wanted to build a Holy Land of sorts in the United States. The idea was that if pilgrims couldn't get to Christianity's holiest sites, then those sites would come to them. The priests envisioned Staten Island as the perfect spot, but when that fell through, they moved their "mountain comes to Mohammed" dream to Washington, where six Franciscan brothers shared a dilapidated mansion, complete with rats, on 44 overgrown acres on a hillside in Brookland. By 1898, the enterprising priests had secured a plan, raised the necessary funds, and had begun work on the new Memorial Church of the Holy Sepulchre. It was modeled after the Hagia Sofia in Istanbul, Turkey, with a replica of the Catacombs of Rome and the Bethlehem Manger beneath—and for the undoubtedly grateful Franciscan brothers, a new friary behind the church.

It's a perfect retreat, juxtaposed with this neighborhood's transitional blocks where houses are either shabby or semi-restored and where police sirens wail all too often. In the early years, the Franciscans ran a farming operation. It has since been replaced by a wooded grotto—where the Stations of the Cross offer an opportunity to pray and reflect—and by a meticulously maintained rose garden encircled by the Rosary Portico. The Portico features 15 tiny chapels, each bearing a plaque with the words of the traditional Catholic prayer "Hail, Mary" which begins "Hail, Mary, full of grace, the Lord is with thee," written in 200 ancient, as well as modern, languages.

*Left:* Worshippers gather for Mass at the Franciscan Monastery's Memorial Church of the Holy Sepulchre in this photograph from 1945. The church is modeled after the Hagia Sofia in Istanbul. *Below:* The Franciscan Monastery's Rosary Portico, with its red-tile roof, surrounds a garden of roses and annuals. The Portico features reproductions of shrines from the Holy Land, making it a perfect spot for prayer and reflection.

# GALLAUDET UNIVERSITY

Every graduate of Gallaudet, the nation's only university for the hearing impaired, receives a diploma signed by the President of the United States, a tradition that began in 1869, when President Ulysses S. Grant signed the diplomas of the university's three graduates in its first class.

The university began in 1856 when Amos Kendall donated two acres of his estate to establish a school. Kendall was a journalist, a wealthy newspaper publisher, a close advisor to President Andrew Jackson, and an associate of telegraph inventor Samuel F. B. Morse, whose wife, Sarah, was hearing impaired. Edward Miner Gallaudet, whose mother was deaf and whose father, Thomas, had earlier operated a school for the deaf, became the institution's first president. At that time, the school went by the unwieldy name of The Columbia Institution for the Instruction of the Deaf and Dumb and Blind.

In 1954, by congressional act, the college was renamed in honor of Thomas Hopkins Gallaudet; university status was granted in 1986. The university has kept to its original mission: providing quality education for the hearing impaired by admitting those students almost exclusively. It also focuses its undergraduate and graduate programs on education and services for the hard of hearing.

Gallaudet is also credited with devising the football huddle. In the 1890s, its star quarterback, Paul Hubbard, hit upon the idea of drawing his deaf teammates closer in order to shield his hand signals from the opposing team—a bit of cleverness that quickly spread to other college teams.

*Right:* Gallaudet University's Chapel Hall, also called the Main Central Building, is considered to be one of the best examples of post–Civil War collegiate architecture in the United States. Designed by Frederick C. Withers, it was completed in 1871.

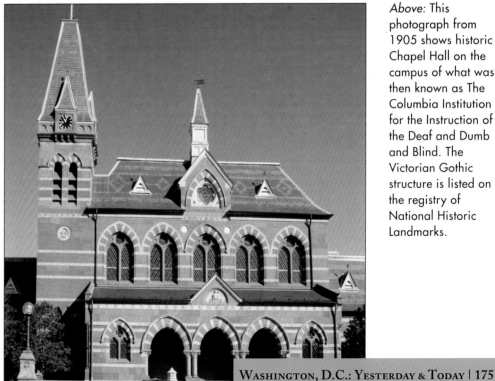

*Above:* This photograph from 1905 shows historic Chapel Hall on the campus of what was then known as The Columbia Institution for the Instruction of the Deaf and Dumb and Blind. The Victorian Gothic structure is listed on the registry of National Historic Landmarks.

Hikers follow the trail at the National Arboretum in spring when more than 70,000 azaleas are in peak bloom.

# NATIONAL ARBORETUM

The National Arboretum sits on more than 440 glorious acres overlooking the Anacostia River on a hillside once known as Mount Hamilton, a former Civil War fortification. The Arboretum (from Latin, meaning "a place of trees") is a federal government-operated research facility. Congress established it in 1927—in an early gesture of "thinking green"—for "the purposes of research and education concerning tree and plant life." Although it's not a park in the usual sense, thousands are drawn here every year, particularly in spring, to hike or drive the 9.5-mile roadway and enjoy the blooming azaleas, dogwoods, and rhododendrons.

That, of course, is not all. Other outstanding features include the Aquatic Garden, which is surrounded by lilies and filled with Japanese koi; the

National Bonsai and Penjing Museum, which showcase the dwarfed varieties of trees and shrubs; and the National Herb Garden, which consists of themed gardens featuring antique roses and herbs.

Recent research efforts have focused on plant tolerance of insects and diseases. To that end, the Arboretum has successfully introduced a disease-resistant American elm, bred specifically to resist Dutch elm disease, which, by the 1970s, had killed all the American elms, as well as a new and hearty hybrid of crape myrtle called 'Natchez', one of 20 new crape myrtle varieties, each named for a Native American tribe. In 2002, the Arboretum embarked on a 20-year master plan of improvements that includes tree-lined walks, an education and visitors center, and still more gardens.

The bonsai collection at the National Arboretum is one of its most popular attractions. It was begun in 1976 with a gift to the American people from Japan's Nippon Bonsai Association to commemorate the bicentennial. Some of the original 53 trees are more than 350 years old. The collection has since grown to include 150 plants, which are housed in three pavilions.

The National Arboretum's Herb Garden features medicinal specimens, cooking herbs, and herbs used for teas and dyes, as well as herbs used by Native Americans and the English colonists. The garden also includes beds of historic and fragrant roses.

## *The Capitol's Columns at the Arboretum*

One of the National Arboretum's best-known attractions isn't a tree, bush, or rare plant specimen, but rather these 34-foot-tall Corinthian columns, originally part of the U.S. Capitol building's east portico. During the 1950s, when the Capitol was undergoing renovations, the sandstone columns were replaced with marble. These columns were then mothballed until the National Arboretum acquired them in the 1980s. Arranged at the foot of a reflecting pool, the columns seem more like relics of ancient Greece or Rome than artifacts of the early American republic. Night lighting adds drama to the columns, a popular stop on the Arboretum's guided five-mile evening tours.

# MARINE BARRACKS

The Marine Corps was founded by the Continental Congress in 1775 and moved from its Philadelphia headquarters to the nation's new capital city in 1800. The barracks were designed by George Hadfield, who also designed Arlington House (the former home of Robert E. Lee and now part of Arlington National Cemetery). The Marine Commandant's House, which was completed in 1806, is the second-oldest public building in Washington (the White House is the oldest) and is still in use today. Between 1904 and 1907, the barracks, the band hall, and the officers' quarters were given a makeover. Essentially, they are today as they were in the early 20th century.

The Marine Band, also known as "The President's Own," is stationed here and has played for every president since John Adams. On summer evenings, the Band and the Drum and Bugle Corps perform on the parade grounds for the public, their spit-and-polish precision stirring patriotism in even the most cynical.

The barracks also was once home to John Philip Sousa, the "March King," who led the band between 1880 and 1892. Sousa was born in 1854 in Washington, one of ten children. Sousa's father enrolled him in the Marines after John, at age 13, tried to run away to join the circus. By the time of his discharge in 1875, Sousa had become an accomplished violinist. Soon he rejoined the Marines in order to conduct and compose for the band. Sousa was as popular then as any rock star today. His best known marches include "The Washington Post March," written as part of a publicity scheme for the newspaper, and "The Stars and Stripes Forever," which is the country's official march. Sousa died in 1932.

A crowd gathers to witness the hanging of Lincoln assassination coconspirators Lewis Powell, David Herold, George Atzerodt, and Mary Surratt, the first woman to be executed by federal order, at the Washington Arsenal on July 7, 1865. The Washington Arsenal, known today as Fort Lesley J. McNair, was established in 1791 on 28 acres at the point where the Potomac and Anacostia rivers meet.

In 1943, female workers at the Washington Navy Yard operate lathes. The Yard employed some 1,400 women during World War II, when conscripted men left a vacuum in the workforce. The Yard itself dates from 1799 and was the Navy's first shore facility, serving as a naval gun factory during both world wars. Today, the Yard houses administrative offices.

The Marine Corps Barracks have been at 8th and I streets in Southeast since 1801.

## The President's Own

The United States Marine Band parades at the barracks in this 1959 photograph. The 60-piece band has been performing for more than 200 years at many state functions, including presidential inaugurals and funerals. The record isn't certain, but the band may have played "Hail to the Chief" for the first time in 1828 during the groundbreaking ceremony for the C & O Canal over which President John Quincy Adams presided. The band performed in New York at the first anniversary of the World Trade Center attacks and with the National Symphony Orchestra at the Kennedy Center. It also offers a popular series of free concerts at venues around Washington and across the country.

# THE ANACOSTIA: WASHINGTON'S OTHER RIVER

The Potomac may be Washington's best-known river, but it isn't the only one. There's also the Anacostia, which divides the city's eastern end. Long neglected, the Anacostia has recently become the focal point of a $12 billion revitalization plan aimed at river clean-up and the beautification of the east and west banks, making the neighborhoods that line them economically and culturally viable for the first time in the city's 200-plus-year history.

The name "Anacostia" derives from the name of a Native American tribe John Smith encountered when he explored the river in 1608. He believed the river to be part of the Potomac, so he named it Eastern Branch, though the Anacostia is a separate waterway, with its headwaters located in nearby Montgomery County, Maryland. (The Potomac's are in West Virginia.) Today, more than half of the Anacostia's watershed is impervious, meaning that paved surfaces, such as parking lots and streets, along with rooftops and other impenetrable surfaces, inhibit natural percolation of rainwater, thus increasing runoff. Add to that the trash, fertilizers, pesticides, and sewage discharge unthinkingly dumped into the river, and it's a wonder the Anacostia has survived at all. In 2007, the Capital River Relief project plucked 50 tons of garbage from Washington's rivers, most of it from the Anacostia, which is only a little more than eight miles long.

The area is slated for extensive commercial and residential development, but built into the plan is a new Anacostia awareness that includes cleanup and beautification. Taking a cue from the National Arboretum and Kenilworth Aquatic Gardens, which front the Anacostia, plans for the river's renewal include a 22-mile trail along both banks, linking the eastern neighborhoods to the National Mall.

### *Frederick Douglass's Cedar Hill*

Frederick Douglass lived in this farmhouse (shown in this undated photograph) from 1877 until his death in 1895. Douglass purchased the home and the surrounding ten acres—called Cedar Hill for the cedar trees once on the lot—for $6,700, a considerable sum at the time. By then, Douglass's career as a public official, a journalist, a publisher, and an influential spokesman for the cause of African Americans and for women's suffrage had secured his position. He was born a slave in 1818 in Maryland and eventually taught himself to read and write. He escaped to work on the Baltimore docks and then fled with his wife, Anna Murray (a freed slave he met in Baltimore), to Massachusetts. In 1882, Anna died, and two years later, Douglass married his secretary, Helen Pitts, creating controversy because she was white. After her husband's death, it was Helen who saw to it that Congress preserve the estate and charter a historical society in Douglass's name. The National Park Service, which acquired the property in 1962, offers tours and special events.

A bust of civil rights pioneer Frederick Douglass occupies a corner of his bedroom at Cedar Hill, his former home. John Van Hook, a Philadelphia architect and real estate developer, built the house in the 1850s. Douglass made several improvements, including adding a library, a new kitchen, and finishing the attic. In all, he expanded the original farmhouse into a 21-room mansion.

The smokestacks of a power plant, part of Washington's Potomac Electric Power Company (Pepco), dominate the skyline along the Anacostia River's marshland near Kenilworth Aquatic Gardens in 1929. The plant is still located there today.

## Anacostia Marshland

Cows drink from a marshland pond along the Anacostia River, with the Capitol building in the background, in 1888. Twentieth-century urbanization gradually replaced the Anacostia's small riverfront farms and destroyed much of its wetlands, once thought to be worthless. Today, the Anacostia's marshlands are making a comeback, thanks to riverfront revitalization that began in the 1990s, which recognizes the value these marshes have in attracting wildlife and aiding in water filtration and springtime flood control.

A kayaker paddles through trash on the Anacostia River. Long-neglected and also a discharge site for Blue Plains, the city's water and sewage facility, the river and its adjacent marshes are slowly being reclaimed.

### Kenilworth Aquatic Gardens

Kenilworth Aquatic Gardens, operated by the National Park Service, has one of the largest water lily gardens in the world. The gardens began when Civil War veteran W. B. Shaw cultivated a dozen lilies in a pond on his 37-acre farm along the Anacostia River. As the lilies grew, and his stock expanded, he and his daughter, Helen Shaw Fowler, began selling their lilies commercially. Helen took over the operation when her father died in 1921 and fought to save this largely unspoiled marshland when the Army Corps of Engineers threatened Shaw Gardens, as it was known, during dredging of the silted Anacostia in the 1930s. In 1938, Helen closed her business, and the National Park Service took over the property. Integral to the Anacostia's wetland system, Kenilworth Gardens today plays a key role as restoration of the long-neglected Anacostia slowly proceeds.

# SOUTHWEST AND SOUTHEAST REINVENTED

In recent years, city leaders have embarked on a new plan for Washington, one that focuses on those underdeveloped parcels that front the Anacostia and include the Southwest waterfront. The plans are so extensive and so visionary that within the next two decades, some see the creation of neighborhoods where none existed before—a mix of commercial and residential use along with new facilities for the federal government.

In 2009, ground was broken for the new headquarters of the Office of Homeland Security on the current site of St. Elizabeths Hospital, with still more development of government facilities at Buzzard Point, on the Anacostia's west shore, and Popular Point, on its east.

Opened in 2008, Nationals Park, home of the Washington Nationals baseball team, serves as temporary anchor while construction proceeds at full-tilt in Southwest, plans for which include a new maritime cultural center and full restoration of the historic fish market. Twenty-two miles of trails will link the east to the Mall and feature parks, courts, playing fields, marinas, public piers, esplanades, and other green spaces. So far, more than $12 billion has been committed, with more on the way, as city planners and architects team up to transform land that had been abandoned or neglected for much of the 20th century.

Except for Georgetown, much of Washington's waterfront has languished, the site of industrial and government installations with access further cut off by the tangle of highways built along its shores in the 1950s and '60s. On top of that, federal, state, and local jurisdictions had to be consulted with every change in the riverscape. But thanks to some enlightened thinking and cooperation among developers, city planners, and various government agencies, Washington's Potomac and Anacostia waterfronts, when completed, should give a whole new meaning to the phrase "down by the river."

St. Elizabeths' 176-acre campus, reserved for the care of the mentally ill, is located on a largely undeveloped site overlooking the Anacostia River (below). Its "N" building is one of 62 historic buildings on the campus and is shown at left, almost 100 years after the hospital opened in 1855. The facility, then called the Government Hospital for the Insane, opened after social reformer Dorothea Dix's campaign drew national attention to the plight of the mentally afflicted. During the Civil War, the hospital also took in the critically wounded. To avoid the stigma of the insane asylum, the soldiers called the hospital St. Elizabeths, the tract's original name.

The Maine Avenue Fish Market on the Southwest waterfront has operated since the early 1800s. When the area surrounding the market was razed in the 1960s to make way for office buildings and a highway, the fishmongers refused to leave, pointing to their original lease which guaranteed them market space for 99 years. Developers relented but forced the market into an undesirable spot beneath an overpass. Current development plans for the historic market call for an up-to-date and expanded facility.

Historic Wheat Row, seen here from the front today, was built in 1795 as part of an early real estate development scheme; it is one of Washington's earliest structures. It survived a wave of redevelopment in the 1950s and '60s, which replaced many of Southwest's modest neighborhoods with a warren of federal office buildings, and has been declared off-limits during the new round of redevelopment. The structure, located along 4th Street in Southwest, was named for John Wheat, one of the original residents.

## LITERARY WASHINGTON

TWO OF WASHINGTON'S MOST CELEBRATED contemporary fiction writers, George Pelecanos and Edward P. Jones, both write about their hometown but in decidedly different ways. Pelecanos—who worked as a line cook, dishwasher, bartender, and women's shoe salesman before publishing his first novel in 1992—is a third-generation Washingtonian best known for his crime novels, such as *Shame the Devil* and *Hell to Pay*. "When I started out," Pelecanos said, "I didn't feel as if Washington, D.C., had been fully represented in literature. And by that I mean the real, living, working-class side of the city." That's an observation that Jones, who also published his first book in 1992, the critically acclaimed short-story collection *Lost in the City*, would likely agree with. Jones grew up in poverty, not far from the Capitol, in some of the city's grittiest neighborhoods and takes as his subject the lives of struggling black Washingtonians who migrated from the South. These were friends and neighbors Jones knew growing up, who, as he said, "lived their lives as if God were watching everything they did." Jones, who labored at the obscure trade journal *Tax Notes* for years before finding literary fame, won the Pulitzer Prize in 2004 for his novel *The Known World*, about an antebellum black Virginia slaveholder. Jones's second story collection, *All Aunt Hagar's Children*, was praised by both *The New York Times* and *The Washington Post* when it appeared in 2006, though Jones has been silent since then. "I write a lot in my head," he says. "I've never been driven to write things down," though when he does, the somewhat reclusive Jones, who lives alone in a tiny apartment in a neighborhood in Northwest, is sure to produce another insightful and pointed tale. Pelecanos—who rides shotgun with nighttime D.C. police patrols and interviews prostitutes, drug dealers, and other criminals—is unlikely to run out of story material any time soon. "I write D.C. novels," he says, "because I live here."

# BASEBALL IN WASHINGTON

September 21, 1961 was a truly bad day in Washington. That was the last day the Washington Senators, the city's beloved baseball team, played at Griffith Stadium. The park opened as National Park Stadium in 1891. It was renamed in 1914 for Senators owner and local businessman Clark Griffith. It was also one of the city's few integrated public facilities, although professional baseball itself remained segregated. When the Senators played away games, Griffith Stadium hosted several African American teams, perhaps the best among them being the Homestead Grays, originally a Pittsburgh team whose eventual Hall-of-Famers included Cool Papa Bell, Josh Gibson, and Buck Leonard.

In 1953, New York Yankee Mickey Mantle hit his legendary 565-foot home run out of Griffith Stadium. But by the 1960s, Griffith Stadium had become home to the Washington Redskins, the city's NFL football team, which eventually moved to the newer RFK Stadium, named for Robert F. Kennedy. In 1966, Griffith Stadium was razed to make way for Howard University Hospital.

In 2008, as part of the first leg of a revitalization plan intended to transform the city's eastern side, the new Nationals Park opened, a 41,888-seat facility which serves as home to the city's new Major League Baseball team, the Washington Nationals, formerly the Montreal Expos.

*A Team by Any Other Name...*

The Washington Senators originally belonged to the National League but folded after the team's 1899 season. When they began play in the American League in 1901, they called themselves the Nationals to avoid any confusion with the previous franchise. However, fans weren't hearing it and continued to call them the Senators. The team was officially renamed the Senators in 1956. *Above:* Washington fans line up outside Griffith Stadium to buy tickets for the 1925 World Series. The Pittsburgh Pirates took the Series from the Senators, four games to three. *Left:* The cover of the Official Souvenir Score Card for the 1933 World's Series featured Joe Cronin, manager of the Washington Nationals (known by fans as the Senators), and Bill Terry, manager of the New York Giants. The Giants won the Series in five games.

Vern Stephens of the Boston Red Sox swings at a pitch in a game against the Washington Senators in 1949 at Griffith Stadium.

## Baseball in Washington

On March 29, 2008, the Washington Nationals played for the first time in their new stadium in an exhibition game against the Baltimore Orioles. The Nats, as the team is known, won. The new Nationals Park offers seating for more than 41,000 fans and has eight escalators, seven elevators, and several conveniently located ATMs, necessary for those essential beer-and-a-dog purchases.

Nationals Park, its official logo shown here, is the new stadium for the Washington Nationals, the city's National League baseball team.

# Index